BRIGHT
NEW IDEAS

Speaking and Listening Games

AGES 5-11

Celia Warren

Author
Celia Warren

Editor
Susan Elliott

Assistant Editor
Jane Gartside

Project Editor
Wendy Tse

Series designer
Joy Monkhouse

Designer
Catherine Mason

Illustrations
Garry Davies

Cover photographs
© Ingram Publishing

Published by Scholastic Ltd,
Villiers House,
Clarendon Avenue,
Leamington Spa,
Warwickshire
CV32 5PR

Printed by Bell & Bain Ltd, Glasgow

Text © Celia Warren 2004

3 4 5 6 7 8 9 0   5 6 7 8 9 0 1 2 3

Visit our website at www.scholastic.co.uk

British Library Cataloguing-in-Publication Data
A catalogue record for this book is available from
the British Library.

ISBN 0-439-97131-4

Acknowledgements
Eric Finney for the use of 'Wilkins' Drop' by Eric Finney
from *Another Third Poetry Book* edited by John Foster
© 1988, Eric Finney (1988, Oxford University Press).
Wes Magee for the use of 'Calling Calling' and 'Summer
Sun' from *The Witch's Brew* by Wes Magee © 1989, Wes
Magee (1989, Cambridge University Press).
Janis Priestley for the use of 'Just One Wish' by Janis
Priestley from *The Works 2* edited by Brian Moses and Pie
Corbett © 2002, Janis Priestley (2002, Macmillan).
Coral Rumble for the use of 'Guess Who' by Coral Rumble
from *The Works* edited by Paul Cookson © 2000, Coral
Rumble (2002, Macmillan).
Jill Townsend for the use of 'Canute's Account' and 'Letter
to My Uncle' by Jill Townsend from *Loony Letters and Daft
Diaries* edited by Paul Cookson © 2003, Jill Townsend (2003,
Macmillan).
Celia Warren for the use of 'The Gingerbread Man' from
Food Rhymes, edited by John Foster © 1998, Celia Warren
(1998, Oxford University Press); for 'This Little Poem' from
Ready for a Picnic by Celia Warren © 2004, Celia Warren
(2004, QED (Quarto Publishing); for 'Left Out' from *Feelings
Poems* edited by John Foster © 1995, Celia Warren (1995,
Oxford University Press);'The Red Arrows', 'I like cows',
'The New Boy', 'The Lion and the Mouse', 'The Fox and the
Crow' and 'The Ant and the Grasshopper' are all previously
unpublished and are all © 2004, Celia Warren.

Contents

Introduction

Speaking and listening are as natural as walking and eating. No wonder then that among the 'firsts' that parents look for in their newborn child, alongside the first tooth and the first step, are the first smile and the first word: two essentials to communication and two natural responses to listening.

'Before we started school we knew all our nursery rhymes. Children today start school knowing none.' Not for the first time do we hear this opinion! Luckily, Early Years teachers are past masters at filling any gaps. Reception children soon become familiar with traditional nursery rhymes, and are able to recite many modern verses and finger rhymes. They increasingly learn many more rhymes and word games from the broadening cultural diversity heard in classrooms today. Such shared rhymes, with actions, refrains and repetition are the perfect vehicle for helping children aged seven and under to speak with increased confidence and enjoyment, a forerunner to independent speech and communication of thoughts, ideas and information.

At Key Stage 1 there are many speaking opportunities, from sharing personal news to playing word games. In particular, the rhymes 'I spy with my little eye', 'Here we go round the mulberry bush' and 'Simon says' all deserve a mention. These rhymes help to develop children's skills of listening and speaking with clarity and confidence. Most infant classrooms have dressing-up boxes that encourage role-play. The younger the child, the less inhibited they are, and the more easily and naturally do speaking and listening opportunities slot smoothly into the timetable.

Using the book
The purpose of this book is to provide easily accessible games and activities, aimed at children from the age of five to eleven, with differentiation to accommodate different age groups and abilities. The activities are designed to support and teach the relevant skills and targets for 'speaking and listening' within the National Literacy Strategy, and complement reading and writing. Given the number of speaking games already used in the infant classroom, the ratio of infant: junior games is weighted slightly towards the junior, Key Stage 2, level. Nevertheless, many are aimed at Key Stage 1 and others can be adapted using the 'Differentiation' suggestions.

This book is aimed at teachers, supply teachers, student teachers and teaching assistants. Half of the games and activities are supported by photocopiable material and activity sheets. The aim of the book is to inspire and inform the user, so that lesson plans can be applied quickly and easily. The activities should dovetail into the existing organisation of most timetables, in whatever style of classroom management. Activities are designed to require minimum preparation and directions, providing time-saving background information and useful prompts. Each activity has a 'Learning objective', with a link to the relevant section of the National Literacy Strategy in which the objective appears.

The activity pages have been organised into four chapters:

- **Speaking**
- **Listening**
- **Group discussion and interaction**
- **Drama.**

Each chapter comprises a number of games and activities, followed by photocopiable pages, when required. The games aim to provide variety in order to involve and develop skills across the age groups, complementing each other and slotting into the structure of the school year and termly objectives.

Building confidence

Someone once said that, as we have two ears and one tongue, we should use them roughly in that ratio! This is a useful suggestion to share with the over-talkative youngster who forgets to listen. In contrast, there are children who seem to practise unduly the old Victorian notions of 'children should be seen and not heard' and 'speak when you're spoken to'. As teachers, we aim to encourage a happy medium. This is, surely, what oral communication is all about: a balance between speaking and listening. Here is where group work and drama score, building confidence in shy children and teaching overly garrulous children to give and take; to think, constructively and carefully, before speaking.

Above all, effective and unambiguous communication is the essential shared ingredient and objective of the games and activities in this book. Fluency and lucidity of speech encourages ease and reliability of understanding; everyday tools that we all need in every area of life.

One final activity that you might like to try, when you have tried all in this book, would be to discuss as a class just a few of the many maxims related to speaking and listening:

Least said, soonest mended

Speak little but speak the truth

Speaking without thinking is like shooting without aiming

Speech is silver, silence is golden

Speak well of your friends and of your enemies nothing

Easier said than done

Two heads are better than one.

Considering the possible necessities that mothered the invention of such sayings may well justify the existence of this book, and of 'Speaking and Listening' as a specific component of our National Curriculum.

CHAPTER 1

Speaking games

AGE RANGE 5–7

LEARNING OBJECTIVE
To memorise and recite a poem and extemporise within the same framework.

CURRICULUM LINKS
NLS: Y1, T1-3.

This little poem

What you need
Whiteboard; marker pen; small sticky notes.

What to do
● Gather the children together so that they are sitting comfortably, with their hands in their laps. Sit in front of them, in the same position.
● Explain that not all poems and stories are in books. Some we keep in our heads. Ask the children for suggestions, prompting if necessary with nursery rhymes and class favourites, and recite them together.
● Include some finger rhymes such as 'Incy Wincy Spider'.
● Now make fists of your hands and invite the children to copy. Ask them to follow your actions as you recite the following poem:

> This little poem I can keep in my hands *(Hold up tightly closed fists.)*
> Sometimes it wriggles and sometimes it stands *(Wriggle fingers; 'stand' hand on three fingers and thumb, with the middle finger extended to suggest the head of a four-legged animal.)*
> It likes to wave; it loves to clap *(Wave and clap.)*
> Then it falls asleep face down in your lap. *(Yawn with hand over mouth after 'Then…'; hands palm-down on laps.)*

● Repeat a couple of times until the words and actions are secure.
● Invite the children to suggest substitutions for the actions words. For example, 'wriggle' might become 'jump' and 'sometimes it stands' might become 'and then it lands', although all substitutions do not need to rhyme!
● Vary the places where the substitutions are made, for example, in the first line replace 'keep' with alternatives such as 'hold', 'hide' or 'squeeze'.
● In pairs, ask the children to experiment with substitutions and choose their favourites.
● Encourage each pair of children to perform the new verses to the rest of the class, making up suitable hand actions to match the new verbs.

Differentiation
For younger children, write out the poem on the whiteboard. Write the verbs on sticky notes so that the children can try them in different positions. Encourage more able children to incorporate rhyme and make further substitutions within the framework of the same rhythm.

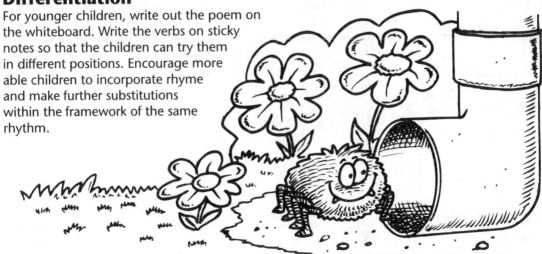

AGE RANGE 5–9

LEARNING OBJECTIVE
To speak coherently and enthusiastically to engage an audience's interest; to answer questions.

CURRICULUM LINKS
Y3, T2-3; Y4, T1-2

Cool dude!

What you need
Access to a library and/or the Internet (if the activity is to include fictional or historical figures); photocopiable page 21.

What to do
● Make one copy of the photocopiable sheet for each child.
● Introduce the activity by telling the children that you have been thinking about someone that you very much admire. Share your enthusiasm for that person, bringing out some of their virtues through anecdote, rather than simple adjectives. For example: 'When she heard I was in bed with the flu, she cancelled her shopping trip and brought me some delicious home-made soup. And she managed to make me laugh with her funny stories!'
● Ask the children why they think you admired her? What personality traits made her appealing? Suggestions might include generosity, thoughtfulness, kindness, sense of humour, selflessness and so on.
● Drawing on examples from shared fiction, encourage the children to talk about characters that they admire, explaining why they admire them.
● Now ask the children to think of a person that they very much admire. Encourage them to examine how the person behaves and presents their personality, rather than if they have, say, a fast car or designer trainers. Would they still admire the person without such outward symbols of success? Encourage the children to study behaviour, manner and attitude, rather than superficial material wealth.
● Ask the children to consider whether it's necessary to like a person in order to admire them. For example, they might admire the bravery of a mountain climber but not like his or her attitude towards other people.
● Explain that you would like them to prepare a two-minute talk about the person that they most admire. Warn them that they must be prepared to answer questions about that person and be aware of the reasons why they admire that person. Challenge them to avoid generalities like 'nice' and 'kind' but find anecdotal examples that demonstrate the person's admirable qualities.
● Give each child a copy of the 'Cool dude!' photocopiable sheet. Explain that they can use the sheet to help them organise their thoughts and as a prompt sheet when they are giving their talk.

Differentiation
Encourage younger children to talk about a favourite person to an adult, who can act as scribe to write cue words to help them speak clearly. Allow them to practise their talk with an adult who can prompt them if they lose the thread. After their introductory talk, invite confident children to take on the persona of their chosen character, and hot-seat them in role.

AGE RANGE 5–11

LEARNING OBJECTIVE
To organise thoughts about issues within their own experience into a coherent argument and speak with conviction.

CURRICULUM LINKS
NLS Y3, T1; Y4, T3; Y5, T1-3; Y6, T2.

Speaker's Corner

What you need
Photocopiable page 22; pencils.

What to do
● Make one copy of the photocopiable sheet for each child.
● Explain that everyone has beliefs that they feel strongly about. Share your own feelings over an issue where you feel people could act more responsibly, for example: 'I dislike it when people leave litter that can hurt or trap small animals'.
● Clarify why this issue makes you cross, upset or annoyed. Maintain eye-contact with the children, using gesture for emphasis and oral techniques to retain their attention, for example, varying your pace or using rhetorical language.
● Ask the children to think of something that they feel strongly about. Prompt if necessary: should parents send them to bed or should they choose their own bedtimes? Is homework a good idea?
● Encourage the children to consider another point of view. Can they anticipate conflicting arguments and counter-arguments to help them to clarify and justify their beliefs?
● Tell the children about Speaker's Corner in Hyde Park, London. Explain that it is a place where people can say exactly what they think. Anyone is free to have their say, though some listeners may heckle if they disagree.
● Invite the children to plan a talk to last about one minute. Give them a guideline of around 150-180 words, and hand out the 'Speaker's Corner' photocopiable sheets, explaining how they can use these to help plan their talk.

● Allow time for the children to practise their talk with a partner. Remind them of techniques that you modelled earlier, for example, audience eye-contact.
● Encourage the partners to play 'devil's advocate', adopting a different point of view, whether or not they agree with the speaker.
● When everyone is ready, invite the children to make their speeches to the group. Forbid heckling until the children get used to speaking and answering invited questions.
● Demonstrate the effect of heckling and encourage children to find methods of adapting their techniques to overcome it.
● Depending on the class dynamics, if you decide to allow heckling, make some ground rules: no interruptions before you give a signal; all interruptions must offer a valid counter-argument rather than simple cries of 'rubbish!'; hecklers must allow time for the speaker to respond.

Differentiation
Invite younger children to make a placard or sandwich board with a catchy slogan and simply prepare answers to questions. Increase the level of heckling for more confident children to encourage quick-thinking.

BRIGHT IDEAS Speaking and Listening Games

AGE RANGE 5–10

LEARNING OBJECTIVE
To speak with increased confidence and clarity while sustaining rhythm.

CURRICULUM LINKS
NLS: Y3, T 1-2; Y4, T2-3; Y5, T2-3.

Who's got the zapper?

What you need
Photocopiable page 23 (one copy per group and one enlarged copy); pens.

What to do
● Display the enlarged copy of the photocopiable sheet at the front of the room.
● Invite five children to join you in front of the class, numbering them: first; second; third; fourth; fifth.
● Ask the children to write their names at the top of the enlarged photocopy, copying them in the appropriate places further down the sheet as a model for group work later.
● Explain that you would like them in turn to read their line from the text. Demonstrate how to read with a steady rhythm.
● After a few practice runs, invite them to attempt to continue the pattern without a written prompt.
● Next, see if they can surprise each other by picking names from their group in a different order. Can the named speaker rise to the challenge and give the response without breaking the rhythm? Remind the children to be thinking who they will pick next as they listen out for their name.
● Give each of the five children a photocopiable sheet and a pen, and ask them to act as leaders for five new groups, with four children joining each respectively.
● Ask the children to fill in their names on the sheet and to practise reading it with the same sustained rhythm. Allow groups to practise and then listen to each group in turn. Discuss ways of making it easier to keep the rhythm smooth. For example, the speaker could make eye-contact in advance with the person that they are going to choose next, so that they can prepare their line in their minds.

Differentiation
Make large copies of the main lines, leaving name-gaps blank, as a prompt for younger children to read. Introduce four slow claps between lines to allow extra thinking time. Play as a whole-class game as the children's skill improves. Challenge children to improvise responses, by rewording while retaining rhythm and rhyme, for example: 'I haven't got the zapper; oh no, not me!'

Speaking and
Listening Games

AGE RANGE 8–11

LEARNING OBJECTIVE
To describe a memorable moment from child's own experience.

CURRICULUM LINKS
NLS: Y4, T1&T3; Y5, T1; Y6, T3.

That moment when...

What you need
Space for the children to talk in pairs.

What to do
● Explain to the children that there are moments in life that stay in our memory very strongly and may even have an impact on our whole lives. These may be moments when we feel something very acutely, such as pain, joy, excitement, embarrassment, humour or fear.
● Help the children to determine that such occasions involve our emotions and offer examples from your own experience. For example, the moment when you heard that you'd got the job you wanted, the first time you held a new baby or the moment when you realised that you knew how to ride a bike but not how to stop!
● Make one example more interesting than the others by adding more detail, such as a variety of tones of voice, facial expressions and moderate gestures.
● Ask the children which of your experiences they enjoyed listening to and why.
● Now invite children to close their eyes and try to picture a special or memorable moment in their own lives. It does not necessarily have to be a dramatic event.
● Organise the children into pairs. Explain that they are going to take turns to tell their partner about 'that moment when…', changing over after a few minutes.
● Encourage the children to think of one of two questions to ask their partner about their story. Keep the questions open so that they elicit greater detail.
● Suggest that the children think about all their senses during the occasion they are recalling. Was the weather warm or cold? Were there any memorable smells or sounds that remind them of that time?
● After a few minutes, bring the class together and invite individuals to tell their story. Ask their partners to say if their story was more interesting now than when they first heard it. Did the questions that they asked help their partner to make their account more detailed, interesting, entertaining or atmospheric?

● Ask the children whose account they think sounded the best-told. Which were the most effective aspects of their story-telling? Is the most interesting event necessarily the most vivid account or vice versa? Can anything be made fascinating if the teller makes it so?

Differentiation
For children who find it difficult to remember any particular event ask them to think about a regular, but relatively ordinary, experience, that acutely involves their senses. This could be the sensation of chocolate melting on their tongue, cold rain dripping down their neck, that moment when … they step into a warm bubble bath or Mum's warm towel after a cold swim. Challenge more able children to turn their account into a story, poem or song.

AGE RANGE 5–11

LEARNING OBJECTIVE
To read or recite with expression, using different voices, including 'narration' voice and facial expression as and when appropriate.

CURRICULUM LINKS
NLS: Y1, T2; Y2, T1-2; Y3, T1-3; Y4, T2; Y5, T2-3; Y6, T3.

Pick a poem

What you need

A selection of poetry books whose contents include poems for more than one voice; photocopiable page 24 (one per pair of children); for younger children 'conversation' nursery rhymes such as 'Baa Baa Black Sheep', 'One Two Three Four Five', 'Once I caught a fish alive', 'Simple Simon' and 'Pussy Cat, Pussy Cat'.

What to do

● Read the poems from the photocopiable sheet to the children, using a variety of intonation according to the speaker.

● Explain the importance of varying the tone, volume and speed as well as clarity, when reading or reciting poems.

● Give a bland, toneless reading of one verse to highlight the difference.

● Ask the children to experiment with different voices as they read a poem such as 'Gingerbread Man'. Can they make their voices sound hard, soft, runny or stiff?

● Re-read the poems inviting the children to join in with the direct speech, changing their voice as appropriate. Introduce the term 'narrator' and explain the function of the narrator in reading words that are not direct speech.

● Organise the children into pairs and give one photocopiable sheet to each pair. Encourage the children to practise a performance of one of the poems from the sheet.

● Listen to some of the performances, pointing out successful features and suggesting areas where they might improve.

● Invite the children to scan the poetry books to find further examples of poems for more than one voice, and prepare one to perform later.

● Encourage the children to experiment with light percussion to emphasise the rhythm in poems that are chants or raps or have strong lyrical beat.

Differentiation

Write lines on separate sheets of paper or highlight in colour-code to help younger children to know when to say their own lines. Add stress marks (/) above appropriate words to help children to retain rhythm and sense. Encourage children with a good sense of timing and rhythm to speak some lines, for example a chorus, in unison. Let polished speakers perform to another class.

AGE RANGE 5–11

LEARNING OBJECTIVE
To read aloud with appropriate emphasis and changes of tone and pace.

CURRICULUM LINKS
NLS: Y1, T2-3; Y2, T2-3; Y3, T1-3; Y4, T1-3; Y5, T1&T3; Y6, T1-2.

My favourite part

What you need
Whiteboard; marker pen; selection of fiction books that children have read recently; a familiar book of your own choice; a chosen, prepared extract indicated by a bookmark; photocopiable page 25.

What to do
● Make one copy of the photocopiable sheet for each child.

● You may wish to spread this activity over two sessions. Begin by introducing the children to your chosen book, giving its title and author.

● Express your enthusiasm for the book and give a brief account of its setting, characters and subject matter.

● Tell the children that you are going to read a short extract which is your favourite part, or one of your favourite parts. Briefly place it in context by explaining, for example, what's just happened and why the character is reacting in this manner, how the characters came to be in this situation and what they have just discovered.

● Read your chosen extract with enthusiasm. Make sure that you make good use of pauses, varying pitch, pace, tone, volume, voice (if appropriate) and emphasis. Make eye-contact with the children as you read.

● Succinctly explain in general terms why you liked your chosen passage. For example, you may have liked the humour, the build-up of tension or the tangible sense of place.

● Ask the children to suggest what it was that made that extract so appealing, for example the use of direct speech, the sudden use of short sentences, the evocative use of adjectives and references to senses and emotions with which the reader may identify.

● Invite the children to choose a book that they have read recently, and to select a favourite part. Limit this to half a page or a couple of paragraphs, depending on the length and style of book and age of child.

● Give each child a copy of the photocopiable sheet and explain that they can make notes on the sheet, giving a short introduction to their chosen extract and the reasons for their choice.

● Demonstrate on the board how to write the opening words and closing words from your own chosen extract, including the page reference for ease of location.

● Allow time for children to practise reading their extract before presenting it to the rest of the class.

Differentiation
Act as scribe for struggling writers. Model reading their chosen passage aloud for them to emulate and copy the text on a separate sheet for children to follow more easily. Invite listeners to question the speaker to find out more about the book. Did they find the story's ending satisfying? Were there any 'boring' parts that slowed down the plot? Have they read other books by the same author?

AGE RANGE 9–11

LEARNING OBJECTIVE
To explain and justify choices; to improvise sentences within specific context with oral dexterity.

CURRICULUM LINKS
NLS: Y5, T1-3; Y6, T1-3

DIY definitions

What you need
Whiteboard; green, black and red pens; dictionaries with etymology; paper; pencils; photocopiable page 26.

What to do
● Make one copy of the photocopiable sheet for each child or pair of children.
● On the whiteboard, write some multi-syllabic words in black, leaving a space underneath each, for example, 'consolidate', 'submariner' and 'advertisement'.
● Ask the children to identify common prefixes and suffixes within each word and to underline them.
● Rewrite the words underneath, using green for any prefix and red for any suffix. Write the remaining syllables in black to clarify the breakdown of the word.
● Explain that the prefixes and suffixes have meaning in themselves, for example, 'pre' and 'ante' mean 'beforehand'; 'post' means 'after' or 'following'. Take the opportunity to explain that 'a.m.' and 'p.m.' mean 'ante meridian' and 'post meridian' (*meridian* meaning midday), hence 'a.m.' is literally 'before midday' – morning.
● Ask the children to find more long words in the dictionaries and to write them down, breaking them up in the same way.
● Explain the word 'definition' to the children. Ask them to note and read aloud the definitions of some of the words that they have looked up.
● Hand out the photocopiable sheets to individuals or pairs of children and read through the sheets with them, answering any questions they may have.
● When the children have completed their photocopiable sheets, explain that you are going to ask each child, or pair of children, to read their favourite nonsense word aloud *without* their definition. Give an example of your own first, for example: displonkify *verb* (without its definition *to get up or cause another to get up*).

displonkify
(dis-plonk-i-fy) [v]

to get up or to cause another to get up.

● Now use your word in a sentence to help show its meaning through context. The word may be slightly altered within grammatical usage, for example: 'When I was waiting on the station platform I was tired, but the Trains Official displonkified me / made me displonkify'.
● Invite the children to guess what your nonsense word might mean, then encourage guessers to put it into a new sentence to show their interpretation.
● Finally, give your definition and explain why you gave the word that meaning. For example, *dis* (a negative), *plonk* (to set down) and *i-fy* (to make).
● Invite the children to have a go themselves, sharing their own nonsense words with the rest of the group!

Differentiation
Rewrite words with syllables hyphenated to help younger children to decipher long words, for example 'dis-plonk-if-y'. Use alphabet letters, divided into colour-coded consonants and vowels and demonstrate how each syllable needs a vowel (or a 'y') usually sandwiched between consonants. Ask more confident children to create and tell a short story, involving all five new words from their worksheet, the context revealing their meaning.

AGE RANGE 5–9

LEARNING OBJECTIVE
To retell a story dramatically, adding detail for greater interest and creating dialogue, speaking audibly and with varying tone of voice and appropriate facial expression.

CURRICULUM LINKS
NLS: Y1,T2-3; Y2, T3; Y3,T3; Y4, T1.

Bare bones

What you need
Photocopiable page 27; whiteboard; marker pens.

What to do

● Make one copy of the photocopiable sheet for each child.
● Tell the children about Aesop, a Greek slave and story-teller who lived more than 2500 years ago.
● Point out that story-telling is older than reading, writing and books. Explain that Aesop's fables were verbally passed down generations and across continents before being written down only two or three hundred years ago.
● Give each child a photocopiable sheet showing the strip cartoon of Aesop's fable, 'The Hare and The Tortoise'.
● Read the captions together. Is this an interesting telling of the story? Would this be how Aesop told the story? Would it be memorable or popular if told so simply?
● Invite suggestions as to how the text could be made more interesting. What are the characters like? How can this be shown by the way they move and speak? Use the pictures to help find words and sentences to 'flesh out' the story and the characters.
● On the whiteboard collect adjectives suggested by the children to describe the characters and setting.
● Using the children's suggestions, scribe an opening paragraph to introduce the characters, setting and situation.
● Discuss what the moral of the story might be. How do the children feel about the characters' behaviour? With whom do they sympathise? How would they feel if they were the tortoise; the hare; an onlooker?
● Find words to describe the characters' personalities, behaviour and emotions, for example: boastful, haughty, arrogant, determined, resolute, strong.
● Challenge the children to involve all their senses. Perhaps the tortoise defies temptation to stop and nibble the sweet smelling grass? Maybe the hare listens to the ground and can hear no footsteps so decides to take a nap?
● Let children share ideas in pairs to write the story in a gripping way. Use the photocopiable sheets to help remind them to pace their stories and arrange the stages of the story into paragraphs.
● Invite the children to retell their stories. Encourage them try to *tell* the story in a lively way and to use their written version only as a prompt.
● Invite the rest of the group to comment and give feedback after they have listened to the stories. How did their efforts improve on the 'bare bones'?

Differentiation
Let younger children act out the roles and scribe their words for them. Provide opening lines for each phase of the story, for example: 'One windy March day, Hare had been bounding energetically around the field all morning…'. Encourage more able children to use thesauruses to find vivid, less commonplace adjectives.

AGE RANGE 5–8

LEARNING OBJECTIVE
To tell an accumulative list-based story from
imagination, adding nouns and adjectives in the
telling; sustaining interest and aiding memory by
using variety of tone, pace, accent, stress, gesture and
so on.

CURRICULUM LINKS
NLS Y1, T1-3; Y2, T1-3; Y3, T2-3.

On a picnic

What you need
Paper; pencil; whiteboard for drawings (optional).

What to do
● Explain to the children that you are going to begin a story and you would like them
to listen carefully.
● Tell them that you would like them to take turns to develop the story, each time
beginning at the start and repeating the story all the way through, adding interesting
details. (*NB* Make a note of each addition as the story grows, just in case everyone loses
track of its progress!)
● Begin by saying, 'We went on a picnic and with us we took sandwiches'.
● Choose a child to suggest what was in the sandwiches, for example, jam. They
should now repeat your opening line, adding their adjective. For example 'We went on
a picnic and with us we took jam sandwiches'.
● Invite the next child to add another adjective, for example, scrumptious (jam
sandwiches). Again, the child must repeat the whole sentence from the start, with both
new adjectives.
● Ask the next speaker to add another item to the list of things that you took on the
picnic, repeating the whole narrative from the beginning: 'We went on a picnic and
with us we took scrumptious jam sandwiches and an umbrella'.
● Continue the story around the class, adding adjectives and nouns accumulatively,
until every child has had a turn. Point out that the word 'and' will move along the list as
it grows, always preceding the final noun.
● Finally, as the story returns to you, tell the children that you are going to end it with
the line, '…but when we got there it started to rain, so we had to run home with …'. At
this point, ask for the children's help in repeating all of the items that were taken on the
picnic, as a group.

Differentiation
Do simple drawings of the items taken as a visual cue for younger children during the
development and retelling process. Challenge more able children to attempt retelling
the whole story alone or in pairs.

AGE RANGE 8–10

LEARNING OBJECTIVE
To speak with sustained rhythm, appropriate stresses and suitably upbeat tone of voice; to improvise within this rhythm between a chorally spoken refrain.

CURRICULUM LINKS
NLS: Y4, T3; Y5, T2-3.

The classroom rap

What you need
Whiteboard; marker pen.

What to do
● Invite the children to help you make up a rap poem that you can all recite together. Tell them that it will belong to them and their school because they will all be in the poem.

● Demonstrate that the chorus will say 'Clap, clap, the Classroom Rap!' If possible, substitute the name of your school, for example, 'Clap, clap, St Peter's Rap!' or 'Clap, clap, the Year Four Rap!' to increase the children's sense of ownership and enthusiasm.

● Give four slow claps as you practise this chorus line altogether, so that the words 'clap', 'clap', 'class' and 'rap', coincide with the strong beats.

● Add a new line with your name in it. For example, 'My name's Miss Bloggs and I like to rap' or 'My name is Ben and I like to rap'.

● Invite one of the children to say the same line, substituting their own name. Write this line on the board, adding a stress mark (/) above each word that requires a strong beat to maintain the one-two-three-four rhythm. For example, the line 'My name is Sanjay and I like to rap' would have stresses over 'name', 'San', 'like' and 'rap'. Point to the words as they are spoken to help develop a sense of rhythm.

● Demonstrate how the weaker beats are almost swallowed to retain the strong four-beat rhythm. Encourage the children to practise.

● Point out how names of different lengths can be accommodated by using an apostrophe. For example, 'my name is' to gain a beat or 'my name's' to lose one. Use name abbreviations if the child is happy to do so.

● Prepare the children to recite their poem all the way through. Give each child a turn to chant their personal line with their own name in it as you point round the class.

● In between each new line chant the 'clap, clap, …' refrain together.

Differentiation
For younger children, model improvised lines. For example, 'I rap in the morning and I rap at night'. Introduce rhymes, ' I rap with Mum and I rap with Dad; I rap when I'm good and I rap when I'm bad'. Write cue cards for insecure children and be ready to join in with their line; alert children to their turn by pointing and saying, 'and NOW it's YOU!' in time with and during the preceding chorus line.

AGE RANGE 8–11

LEARNING OBJECTIVE
To read at an appropriate pace, pausing at commas
and full-stops, to retain meaning.

CURRICULUM LINKS
NLS Y4, T1-3; Y5, T2-3; Y6, T1-3.

Pauses and punctuation

What you need
Whiteboard; pens; pencils; paper; photocopiable page 28 (one per pair of children).

What to do
● On the board write the following sentence: 'We stopped waiting at the station'.
● Read the sentence aloud and discern its meaning, that is that the act of waiting was terminated.
● Now insert a comma between 'stopped' and 'waiting'. Remind the children that a comma requires a short pause and then read the newly punctuated sentence aloud.
● Ask the children how the comma alters the meaning of the sentence. If the sentence were spoken by, say, train drivers, which punctuation would allow passengers to board the train and which wouldn't?
● Ask the children to copy the following words from the board three times, one below the other: 'Someone moved a little head raised a dust settled'.
● Explain that the words could form one, two or three sentences, depending on where full-stops, commas and capital letters are added. Invite the children, in pairs, to read the words aloud and experiment with punctuation so that each line makes grammatical sense and says something different. For example: 'Someone moved a little, head raised. A dust settled' or 'Someone moved. A little head raised a dust, settled' and so on.
● Invite a few children to read their sentences aloud and discuss the change in meaning. Which sentence sounds the most sensible? Why?
● Before distributing the photocopiable sheets, explain that the passages on the page may not, at first, make sense. The children may need to read them more than once.
● Organise the children into pairs and give one photocopiable sheet to each pair. Ask the children to read the paragraphs aloud to each other, adding punctuation so that the words make sense.
● Now invite them to re-read the words to each other, pausing at their commas and full-stops, to check that they have added them correctly.
● Encourage the children to read their sentences aloud to the class when they think they can do so with meaning. Invite the rest of the group to offer suggestions for improvement or to achieve variation of meaning.

Differentiation
Give less able children a selection of large print, short sentences, for example, 'We waited for the queen bees humming'; 'Where we were blue buses ran by'. Challenge more able children to invent ambiguous sentences with no punctuation, swapping with partners to try and untangle the meaning.

AGE RANGE 7–11

LEARNING OBJECTIVE
To use story language in a collaborative story creating cue cards to help retell the story.

CURRICULUM LINKS
NLS Y3, T1; Y4, T2; Y5, T2; Y6, T1.

Narrating by numbers

What you need
Five or six dice; 25 to 30 cue cards (approximately A6 size) and a pencil for each group.

What to do
● Divide the children into groups of six. Allocate numbers one to six within each group, explaining that 'Number one' will act as scribe.
● Give each scribe 25 to 30 cue cards and a pencil, and distribute one dice to each group.
● Explain that the children are going to tell a story, making it up as they go along. A shake of the dice will decide whose turn it is to carry on the story.
● Start an open-ended storyline which includes one or two characters and a location, for example, 'One day Jack and Alice were walking beside the canal'.
● Ask the scribes to make notes on the cue cards for each new sentence, numbering them in case they get dropped. Keep the notes brief, for example 'Jack, Alice, canal path'.
● Shake a die and ask the owners of the number, in each respective group, to continue the story. This will mean that each group has the same opening sequence, but will take the story in various directions.
● When the second speaker has added a line to the story, he or she must shake the dice to determine who goes next from their group.
● After every five turns the last speaker should shake the dice to determine who will recap the story so far, using the cue cards to help.

● Demonstrate this yourself showing how, in recapping, more detail may be added, or slight amendments made, to improve the story-telling and the plot development. For example, 'The children saw a windmill' might instead become 'The children saw the arms of a deserted windmill turning'.
● Return the cue cards to the scribe so that they can adjust and update the notes.
● If, after several turns, any number has not been thrown in any group, ask the non-contributor to do the next recap.
● After all cue cards have been used, allow a few minutes for the children to modify and refine their story before choosing a story-teller from each group to tell their story to the class.
● As a follow-up group activity, discuss how each story might end, allowing groups to offer constructive comments on other groups' contributions.

Differentiation
Write opening phrases on the board, such as 'Suddenly', 'After a while', 'Before long' and so on. Have an adult helper act as scribe for slow writers or younger children. Encourage more able children to add direct speech and extra description to their narrative.

AGE RANGE 5–7

LEARNING OBJECTIVE
To give an audible account of a daily event in children's lives, adding details of interest and answering questions.

CURRICULUM LINKS
NLS Y1, T1; Y2, T1.

My journey to school

What you need
A safe, open space.

What to do
● Ask the children whether they think that their journey to school is the same every day. Invite a child who raises their hand to tell everyone about their journey.
● Ask questions and invite more from the class. How busy were the roads? What was the weather like? Were many people carrying umbrellas / wearing sunglasses? Did you see any animals or birds on the way? What were they doing? Was there a long queue at the bus-stop?
● Encourage the child to retell her or his story, incorporating some of the answers to add detail and interest. Ask if the journey really *was* just the same as yesterday's journey? Suggest that tomorrow's might be different again.
● Invite the children, in pairs, to tell their partner about their journey to school. Encourage them to make it as interesting as possible and to answer their partner's questions with details.
● Ensure that the partners are listening and that they do not interrupt with questions. However, they can ask their questions at the end. Devise a signal, such as a clap, to indicate when to change turns.
● After a short while, gather the children together. Explain that they have all been telling their stories in the first person. Remind them of the first child's telling. Model retelling parts of their story in the third person, using the child's name and personal pronouns such as he/she; his/her. Ask the children to identify these changes.
● Ask the listeners to say whether they found their partner's story interesting. Who thinks they listened so well to the story that they could retell it in the third person? Choose a volunteer or select a child who you feel has listened well to retell their friend's story in the third person.
● Ask the 'owner' of the story if they feel it was a fair and accurate account. Was it interesting? How could it have been made even better?
● Challenge the children to look for something that they have never noticed before on their journey to school tomorrow.

Differentiation
Ask diffident children to tell their story to an adult who may suggest ways of adding detail and change of tone, speed, volume and so on. Use the exercise to develop creative writing for more able children. Encourage them to add a fantasy detail to their journey and to use this as the springboard for a story.

Cool dude!

● Complete these details about the person you most admire.

Name of person: _____

Approximate date of birth: _____

Job or profession: _____

His/her interest or hobby: _____

How you met or know him/her: _____

What he/she looks like:_____

An example of why you admire him/her: _____

_____

_____

Something that you will never forget about him/her: _____

_____

Speaker's Corner

● Imagine that you have just one minute to tell the world what you think about an issue that you feel strongly about. How can you make your point in a strong way so that you convince others? Think about the example below or use an opinion of your own.

● Use language that will persuade listeners to agree with you. Make notes below and then practise your talk ready for Speaker's Corner. Be ready to 'defend your corner' if people disagree.

We should be allowed to bring pets to school with us!

Yes - my dog could come on cross country

What if pets are dangerous and escape?

Some of us might be allergic to your pet

My Slogan

I think _____

Three reasons why I think this: _____

_____

_____

An example to back up my argument:

_____

Some people might disagree and say that

or that _____ but

I think _____

Who's got the zapper?

1st speaker .... 2nd speaker ----------------- 3rd speaker ─────────

4th speaker ═══════════ 5th speaker — — — —

● Number yourselves from 1 to 5 and write your names on the lines above and below. Make sure you match it to the correct line pattern. Now read the rhyme below, taking turns.

1st:	Who's got the zapper for the old TV?	5th:	I haven't got the zapper for the old TV.
2nd:	_____ 's got the zapper for the old TV.	4th:	Then who's got the zapper for the old TV?
3rd:	I haven't got the zapper for the old TV.	5th:	.... 's got the zapper for the old TV.
2nd:	Then who's got the zapper for the old TV?	1st:	I haven't got the zapper for the old TV.
3rd:	═══════ 's got the zapper for the old TV.	5th:	Then who's got the zapper for the old TV?
4th:	I haven't got the zapper for the old TV.	1st:	----------------- 's got the zapper for the old TV.
3rd:	Then who's got the zapper for the old TV?	2nd:	I haven't got the zapper for the old TV.
4th:	— — — — 's got the zapper for the old TV.		

● Carry on the game, trying to keep the rhythm smooth and even. After a while, start the rhyme again, this time slotting in anyone's name from your group when it is your turn.

BRIGHT IDEAS Speaking and Listening Games

Pick a poem

Gingerbread Man
'Gingerbread's too hard,'
said the Gingerbread Man,
'I'd rather be made of marzipan.'

'Marzipan's too soft,'
said the Marzipan Man,
'I'd rather be made of strawberry jam.'

'Strawberry jam's too runny,'
said the Strawberry Jam Man,
'I'd rather be made of plain meringue.'

'Meringue's too stiff,'
the Meringue Man said,
'I'd rather be made of gingerbread!'

© Celia Warren

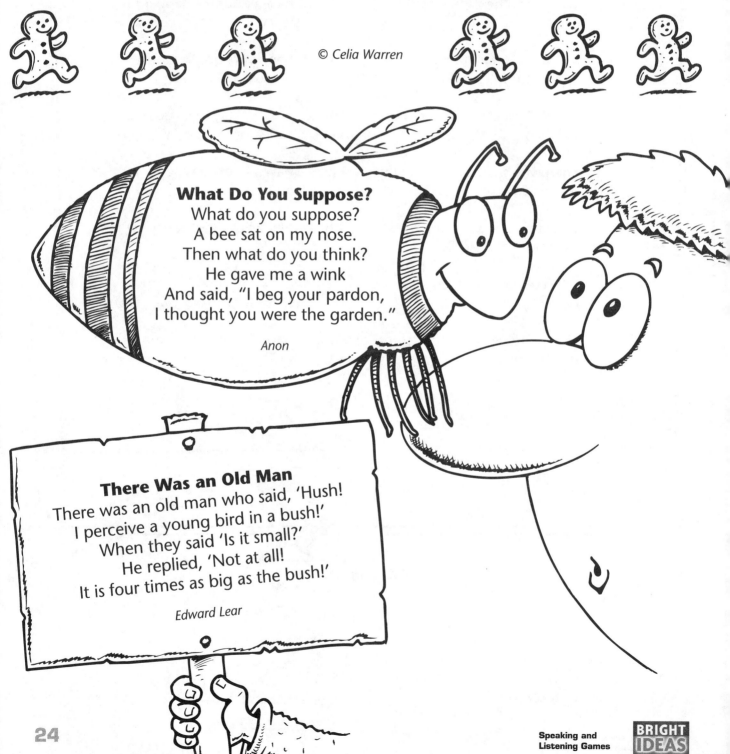

What Do You Suppose?
What do you suppose?
A bee sat on my nose.
Then what do you think?
He gave me a wink
And said, "I beg your pardon,
I thought you were the garden."

Anon

There Was an Old Man
There was an old man who said, 'Hush!
I perceive a young bird in a bush!'
When they said 'Is it small?'
He replied, 'Not at all!
It is four times as big as the bush!'

Edward Lear

Speaking and
Listening Games

BRIGHT IDEAS

My favourite part

Reference notes

Title: _____

Author: _____

Extract

Page number: _____

Begins with the words: ' _____

Ends with the words: ' … … _____

Context (Who? Where? Why?)

The story is about: _____

What has just happened: _____

Introduction notes

I have chosen this extract because _____

I especially like the way _____

DIY definitions

Here are some prefixes:	**Here are some suffixes:**
dis un con de re ad	ment ate tion ism ish ance
com sub pre post ante	tive ise ness less itude ic y

● Mix these prefixes and suffixes with short, one-beat words to invent multi-syllabic nonsense words. The small words may be real or nonsense, for example, dish, bish, mat, grat, bed, thed, wig, stigg, troop, floop.

funfoggitism (fun-fogg-it-ism) [noun]
the art of speaking in riddles

● Neither the above word nor its meaning is real. It is made up. Sometimes parts of the words may suggest a definition: just for fun you can talk in an unclear, foggy way to make what you are saying unclear, like a riddle.
● Adding 'ism' makes it into a noun. Notice how, when the small words and suffix are joined together, the 'y 'in foggy changes to 'i' (foggi) to conform to English spelling conventions.

● Here are more made-up words. Make up definitions for them:

disflagment [noun] means_____

subspaggify [verb] means to _____

● Now make up some new nonsense words. Decide what sort of word each is, for example, a noun, verb or adjective. Now decide what each new word means. Write its definition below.

_____ . . . means_____

_____ . . . means_____

_____ . . . means_____

_____ . . . means_____

_____ . . . means_____

Speaking and
Listening Games

Bare bones

The Hare and the Tortoise

1. Hare could run faster than anyone, especially Tortoise.

2. Tortoise was slower than anyone, especially Hare.

3. Fast Hare thought it would be funny to have a race with slow Tortoise. He was sure he would beat him.

4. Tortoise knew Hare was showing off. Even though Tortoise was slow, he agreed to the race.

5. Hare was soon so far in the lead that he stopped for a rest. He thought he had time for a sleep and would still beat Tortoise.

6. Tortoise kept going without stopping for a rest. He overtook the sleeping hare and, in the end, he won the race.

Pauses and punctuation

● Read through the following paragraph aloud with a partner. Add punctuation such as commas, full-stops and capital letters so that it makes sense.

The children built a sandcastle they thought it would be good
to decorate it with small shells Mum bought them each an ice-cream
one was chocolate and vanilla and the other was
a strawberry ice-cream wearing a swimsuit
Mum sunbathed while they splashed happily
in the sea as jellyfish floated near the shore they had to take care
not to get stung at last they left sand between their toes.

● Now read this sentence. Can you add commas so that it makes sense?

Caesar entered on his head
his helmet on his feet
his sandals in his hand
his sword in his eye
an angry glance.

Draw how you think Caesar really looked.

Speaking and
Listening Games

BRIGHT IDEAS

CHAPTER 2

Listening

AGE RANGE 6–9

LEARNING OBJECTIVE
To consider each other's ideas and suggestions, working as a whole class to generate ideas for creative writing.

CURRICULUM LINKS
NLS: Y2, T3; Y3, T1–2; Y4, T1.

Magic mittens

What you need
A large pair of mittens (alternatively, use a pair of Wellington boots and call the activity 'Wishing wellies'!).

What to do
● Seat the children in a circle. Tell them that you have a pair of magic mittens or, at least, you are pretending that they are magic. Explain that whoever is wearing the magic mittens can do something special; something they couldn't do before.
● Begin the game by putting on the mittens yourself. Give some realistic, if not instantly attainable, examples and some fantasy ones. For example: 'When I wear my magic mittens I can play the piano; I can reach through solid walls; I can bake beautiful cakes; I can catch falling stars; I can do perfect handstands; I can mend broken bones.'
● Point out that all of these activities involve using your hands. (If you are using 'wishing wellies' allow them to take you somewhere that you have never been before. Use real and fantasy examples such as the middle of the desert or the planet Zog.)
● Tell the children that you are going to pass on the mittens around the circle. When it is their turn to put them on, they should decide what they will be able to do that they couldn't do before. Ideas can only be voiced by the person wearing the mittens!
● Give the mittens to a child who is keen to begin and, thereafter, pass them clockwise around the circle.
● When everyone has had a turn, tell the children that they are going to plan a story. Discuss which ideas they liked best. Perhaps someone suggested a location for their story, or a situation. Explore plot possibilities. Use the hypothetical 'What if…?' to lead from the children's own experience to their imaginations.
● While you are discussing suggestions, explain how a plot needs to include a problem and a resolution. Which one or more of the talents provided by the magic mittens could be useful to solve a problem in a central character's life?
● Encourage lateral thinking through repeating 'What if…?' at intervals. For example, a character who can mend broken bones could be very useful to someone who had broken a bone and could not get to a hospital. Where might they be? Who might they be? Rather than an ordinary person, what if it were a giant? Or an animal? Or perhaps a dragon?
● Make sure everyone's ideas are heard and their merits recognised.

Differentiation
For younger children consider things one can really use one's hands for before introducing the 'magic mittens'. Let older children plan their own stories after initial group discussion.

AGE RANGE 9–11

LEARNING OBJECTIVE
To distinguish between formal and informal speech and identify words or phrases that indicate context change; to retain meaning while changing words.

CURRICULUM LINKS
NLS: Y5, T1, T3; Y6, T1–3.

Translators

What you need
The 'Translators' photocopiable sheet on page 43; dictionaries; thesauruses.

What to do
● Make one copy of the photocopiable sheet for each pair of children.
● Remind the children that when you call the register you say, 'Good morning' and they respond similarly. This is a formal greeting. Now ask them to imagine you are casual friends meeting.
● Call various informal greetings and ask the children to echo your greetings, for example: Hi, John!; Howdie, Simin!; Yo, Leanne!; Watchyer…!; Hello…!; Now then…!; Eh-up!… and so on.
● Point out that it sounds funny when we use casual language in a formal situation. Equally, it would seem odd if the children's mums were to wake them up with the words, 'Good morning, sir!' or 'Good day to you, madam! Are you quite refreshed?'.
● Tell the children that they are going to be translators, changing speeches from formal to informal English, and vice versa, just as if it were a different language.
● Ask the children to put their hands up if they can translate the following phrases into less formal language and, if possible, fewer words, while retaining the meaning:
    Would you mind averting your gaze?
    My energy levels are insufficient.
    Is he unable to complete the task?
    Today's climatic conditions are distinctly inclement.
    Shoppers are respectfully requested not to handle the goods.
    You are advised to telephone if you require assistance.
● Organise the children into pairs and give one photocopiable sheet to each pair. Explain that the characters on the sheet are often saying the same thing but they have worded it differently: one formal; one informal. The children must read the phrases aloud and match up the pairs according to meaning.
● Ask the children to decide who is speaking. Encourage them to read aloud in appropriate voices to help them to devise a plausible situation.
● Invite the children to choose two characters and make up a short scenario highlighting their different styles of speech and placing the printed dialogue in context. For example, a formal warning could be given over a tannoy before airline officials confiscate a knife from a passenger, who objects. Invite the children to improvise with their partner before writing a script with a simple setting. Use thesauruses and dictionaries where necessary.

Differentiation
Read aloud to less confident readers, adopting different voices to aid recognition of the different styles of speaker. Suggest characters and context for the children to work on. Challenge more able children to develop their scenario into a short comedy sketch.

Speaking and Listening Games

AGE RANGE 7–11

LEARNING OBJECTIVE
To listen to others, share ideas and follow instructions.

CURRICULUM LINKS
NLS: Y3, T1; Y4, T3; Y5, T1; Y6, T3.

Obstacle race

What you need
A hall or playground; small equipment such as balls, hoops and beanbags.

What to do
● Warm up by playing some team games. Begin with a simple team race. Line up in teams. At a given command, the front runner should spring to touch a beanbag several metres away. They then race back and tag the next in line before joining the back. Continue until everyone in the line has had a turn.

● Follow on with a game that uses equipment such as passing the ball overhead or under legs to the back player, who runs to the front and continues. The first team to complete and sit cross-legged is the winner.

● Now, invite each child to choose one piece of small equipment and then return to their team.

● Tell the teams that you would like them to devise an obstacle race using at least some of the equipment. Give an example, such as running, stepping into hoop and lifting it over head before moving on to beanbag, to be carried on head to next obstacle, and so on.

● Tell the children you would like them to be inventive with the equipment and involve all parts of their body, for example, five hops with a beanbag balanced on the other foot.

● Encourage the children to involve different movements between obstacles, such as forward or backward rolls, stretching and curling. Make sure they listen to each other's ideas and involve everybody in their planning.

● Give children time to try out their obstacle race.

● After a given time, allow each team to describe and then demonstrate their race.

● Invite feedback from the rest of the group, encouraging the children to question any instruction that is unclear.

● Encourage the teams to discuss changes to their race, in response to the comments from the rest of the group.

● Take a vote on which obstacle race most of the children would like to take part in competitively. Invite them to give reasons for their choice.

● Finally, let everyone join in with the race that was voted the favourite!

Differentiation
Take suggestions from the whole class to devise a basic obstacle race. When the children return to their teams ask them to substitute one thing from the basic race to change its format slightly.

AGE RANGE 9–11

LEARNING OBJECTIVES
To ask appropriate questions and listen to others; to recognise homophones.

CURRICULUM LINKS
NLS: Y5, T2; Y6, T3.

Lollipop

What you need
No equipment needed.

What to do
● Seat the children in a circle. Ask children to think of words that sound the same but have different meanings and spellings, for example, 'bare' and 'bear'.

● Demonstrate that, without seeing the written word, we can tell its meaning from context. For example, 'When I climbed into the shower I was completely bare'; 'He was growling like a bear'.

● Tell the children that you are going to repeat those two sentences but, instead of saying 'bare' or 'bear' you are going to substitute the word lollipop. So the sentence would be 'He was growling like a lollipop'.

● For practice, say another sentence where the word 'bear' or 'bare' will be substituted by 'lollipop' and ask the children to guess which spelling of 'bare' or 'bear' it is. For example, 'I can't lollipop the taste of onion'.

● Introduce the concept of the game by telling the children that you are going to think of another pair of homophones. They may ask you up to five questions and you have to use one of the words in your answer, substituting 'lollipop' to represent the homophone. Your answers will be contrived to use one of the words.

● So, for example, if they asked what you had for breakfast, you could choose the homophones 'pear' and 'pair'. Your reply could be, 'I had a lollipop of boiled eggs' or 'I had toast followed by a nice juicy lollipop'.

● Someone might guess the homophone straight away or it may take all five sentences before they guess. Whoever puts their hand up and makes the first correct guess wins.

● Now involve the children in choosing the homophones. Whoever guessed correctly last time should leave the room, while the rest of the group chooses two more homophones.

● Call the child back and invite him or her to ask five questions of different members of the class. They can make a guess at the answer at any point. The last speaker leaves the room next and becomes the guesser.

Differentiation
Be prepared to offer homophones if the children cannot think of many. Some suggestions include: hair/hare; meet/meat; see/sea; choose/chews; steal/steel; shore/sure. As the children improve at the game, try homophones with more than two meanings, for example, poor/pour/paw.

AGE RANGE 8-11

LEARNING OBJECTIVE
To present arguments following the conventions, formal language and structure of a debate; to manage disagreements; to take notes when listening.

CURRICULUM LINKS
NLS: Y4, T3; Y5, T1 & T3; Y6, T2.

Pros and cons

What you need
The 'Pros and cons' photocopiable sheet on page 44; whiteboard; pens; voting slips with two tick boxes labelled 'for' and 'against'; ballot box made from a shoebox with a slit cut in the lid.

What to do
● Tell the children that you want to know what they think about an issue. For example, should infants and juniors share a playground or have separate outdoor play areas? Should children be allowed to bring money to school?

● Ask individuals to stand when they speak so that the rest of the group can hear them clearly.

● Use the term 'debatable' and invite counter-arguments from the group.

● Encourage the children to put themselves 'in someone else's shoes'; a graphic metaphor that will help them to identify with others.

● Invite the children to join in a class debate.

● Explain the structure of a debate. Talk about the roles of proposers, seconders, opposers, floor speakers and chairman. Use the formal, polite language of debate and remind the children that everyone must speak 'through' the chair by addressing Mr or Madam Chairman. The first speaker will present the argument in favour of or against the proposal, the seconder will highlight the proposer's/opposer's main points, before the proposer/opposer summarises. At the end of the debate, the chairman will thank speakers, announce the close of debate and invite listeners to consider both arguments before voting.

● Suggest that everyone considers the pros and cons, whether they support the proposal or not. This will help them to formulate questions and answers.

● Brainstorm a list of issues and write them on the whiteboard. As a group, decide which issue to debate.

● Allocate the roles of chairman, proposer and so on. Allow time for the children to organise their thoughts, considering counter-arguments to help them plan their speech.

● When everyone is ready, give out the photocopiable sheets to be used for taking notes during the debate.

● Begin your debate! If necessary, keep things on track by taking the role of chairperson yourself.

● After the debate, invite the children to cast their votes using the appropriate voting slip, and to post it in the ballot box.

● Appoint vote-counters, ensuring that they give the result only to the Chairman to announce.

Differentiation
Invite more confident children to take the role of chairperson. Help less confident children to take notes and structure questions.

Speaking and Listening Games

AGE RANGE 6–9

LEARNING OBJECTIVE
To follow instructions accurately, asking for clarification if required.

CURRICULUM LINKS
NLS: Y2, T1–2; Y3, T2; Y4, T1.

Carbon copies

What you need
Pencils; shape templates; coloured crayons (optional); A4 white paper; clip boards; an A4 drawing based on the diagram below.

What to do
● Give each child a sheet of A4 white paper. Ask them to place it on the table in front of them so that it is landscape.
● Explain they are going to follow instructions to try to create a 'carbon copy' of an unseen drawing.
● Ask them to fold their paper in half horizontally and open it out, then do the same vertically, so that the fold lines divide the page into quarters.
● Describe to the children what they must draw, giving each instruction separately and using appropriate vocabulary. For example, 'In the bottom left-hand quarter draw a big square with a smaller square inside it.'
● Invite the children to ask questions, such as 'How big is it?' Use comparatives to reply.
● Let children compare their finished drawings with yours. Discuss how successfully they followed your instructions. Where might they have improved? Could the instructions have been clearer? What questions would have helped?
● Distribute plain sheets of paper and shape templates. Ask the children to arrange the shapes on their page to create a pattern and draw around them in pencil or crayons.
● Tell the children that they can use individual shapes more than once, but limit the total number of components in the whole picture. Remind them that they will need to describe their picture, so they should avoid overlapping shapes.
● Ask each child to name their picture, then attach it to a clip board.
● Keeping their pictures obscured, encourage the children to find a partner from a different table and to sit on chairs placed back to back so they cannot see each other. The listener in each pair should clip a blank piece of paper, folded in quarters, on top of their drawing. The speaker will need to keep their drawing hidden from the listener.
● Invite the speakers to describe their drawings to their partners. The listeners should draw freehand or, alternatively, use shape templates.
● Remind listeners that there should be no peeping at the drawings, but they can and should ask questions.
● When each pair has finished, let them compare the copies with the originals before swapping roles.

Differentiation
Modify your drawing according to children's age and ability and spread the activities over two sessions. Divide more confident children into groups in which just one articulate child acts as speaker to five listeners.

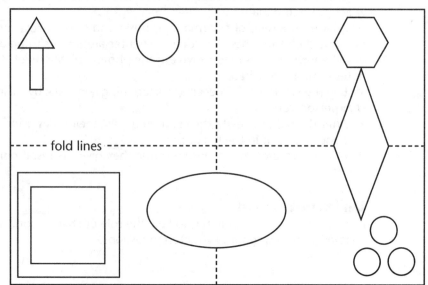

fold lines

34

AGE RANGE 9–11

LEARNING OBJECTIVE
To identify meaning conveyed by metaphorical language and examine its effectiveness; to create and read aloud their own examples; to criticise the effectiveness of each other's contributions.

CURRICULUM LINKS
NLS: Y5, T1–2; Y6, T1–2.

Guess who?

What you need

The poem 'Guess who?' on page 45; thesauruses; paper; pencils.

What to do

● Make one copy of the photocopiable sheet for each pair of children.

● Introduce the concept of kennings. Ask the children if they can guess to which part of the body you are referring to if you say 'my bread basket' (stomach); 'scent sniffer' (nose) or 'word cage' (brain). Explain how two words work together to create a picture, or metaphor, involving the body-part's function.

● Reinforce the concept by inviting the children to make up kennings for hair, eyes, neck, and heart. Discuss which kennings work best and why. Note that kennings avoid using the real word, for example, 'puddle-paddlers' for feet rather than 'foot-paddlers'.

● Give one photocopiable sheet to each pair of children. Challenge them to work out who the poem is about by working out the kennings in the poem.

● When the children offer suggestions, make sure that they can explain their thoughts by reference to the text. For example, 'Music maker'; Henry VIII was a renowned composer, and the tune 'Greensleeves' is attributed to him.

● Working individually or in pairs, ask the children to choose a person about whom to construct a list poem. Each line must be a two-word kenning that sums up some aspect of the person. They may choose someone famous, living or dead, or a generic character such as a police officer or builder. Tell them to keep their choice secret, so that you can play a guessing game later.

● After about ten minutes, invite the children to share single-line examples that they are particularly pleased with. Invite criticism of their strengths and take suggestions for improvement from the rest of the group. If the kennings were too easily guessed or too obscure, how might they be improved?

● Encourage the children to use their best kennings to craft into a list poem. When everyone is ready, invite individuals to read their finished poems aloud. Remind the rest of the group to listen carefully and put their hands up if they can guess who it is. Ensure that they can justify their guesses by reference to the kennings.

Differentiation

Challenge skilful children to make their poems rhyme. Suggest that less confident children write about someone they know well, drawing on personal observation, for example, their mother shopping. Does she use a trolley? Does she push or pull it? Use alliteration and a thesaurus to encourage more vivid descriptions, such as 'trolley trailer'!

AGE RANGE 5–8

LEARNING OBJECTIVE
To listen to a story and retell it in own words; to create and use picture cues; to discuss and predict possible endings.

CURRICULUM LINKS
NLS: Y1, T1–3; Y2, T1–2; Y3, T1–3.

Picture it

What you need
The 'Princess Polly' photocopiable sheet on page 46; pencils.

What to do
● Make one copy of the photocopiable sheet for each child.
● Explain that you are going to tell the story of Princess Polly. The children must listen carefully as, at intervals, you will stop for them to draw a picture showing what has happened. Distribute the photocopiable sheets and pencils.
● Ensure that all pencils are untouched and maintain eye contact with the children as you begin:

Princess Polly wanted to find a handsome prince. She tried pricking her finger on an old spinning wheel. She wanted to go to sleep for a hundred years. 'Ow!' Princess Polly put a plaster on her finger. She was wide awake.

● Allow time for the children to draw a picture in the first box on their sheets. Ask them to put their pencils down, then continue:

Next, Princess Polly tried kissing a frog. Nothing happened, so she let it go. Plop! She tried again. Still nothing happened. (No wonder – it was the same frog!) The frog washed his face. Princess Polly washed her face, too. 'No handsome princes,' she said.

● Ask the children to illustrate this next episode in their second box. Remind them to put their pencils down, then continue:

After that, Princess Polly found some old clothes. They were torn and dirty. She put them on, got a broom and began to sweep the room. She hoped a fairy godmother would appear. She looked out of the window; through the door; even up the chimney. No luck!

● Pause so that the children can draw in the third picture box, then go on:

'Oh, blow!' said Princess Polly. Even as she spoke, a sudden gust of wind made the door swing open and in blew…

● Stop and ask the children to discuss possible endings. What might happen next? After discussion, read the ending and ask them to draw a final picture:

And in blew… a big hairy dog. He knocked Princess Polly off her feet. She stood up, giggling as the dog licked her. 'Who are you?' she said. A disc dangled from the dog's collar. 'Prince,' she read. 'So that's your name! Now I need look no further. You are my handsome Prince.' And they both lived happily ever after.

● Ask individuals to retell the story, making good use of their voices and using their picture cues as prompts.

Differentiation
Draw a simple matchstick figure of Polly for younger children to copy. Let more able children add captions and thought bubbles to develop a strip cartoon.

AGE RANGE 7–11

LEARNING OBJECTIVE
To listen attentively and ask questions; to make judgements based on understanding; to listen and respond using appropriate language and tone of voice.

CURRICULUM LINKS
NLS: Y3, T1–2; Y4, T2; Y5, T1; Y6, T1.

Two's company

What you need
The 'Two's company' photocopiable sheet on page 47 (simplify the sheet for younger children if necessary); pencils; paper; whiteboard; marker pen.

What to do
● You may wish to spread this game across two sessions, working with small groups of children.
● Explain that you are going to play a matchmaking game. Give each child a photocopiable sheet and encourage them to complete the fact file about themselves. To disguise their identity, they must invent a pseudonym. Suggest that they choose the name of a pet or favourite television character to help them remember their pseudonyms.
● Collect the sheets and list the pseudonyms on the board before redistributing the fact files randomly. (Ensure that children do not get their own fact file back.)
● Give each child a blank sheet of paper.
● Allow a few minutes to read the fact files, then ask each child to speak for just thirty seconds about the person whose fact file they have, choosing the most significant and interesting points.
● Ask the listeners to write the name of the pseudonym and make brief notes alongside, for example, 'likes cinema, sporty?'. Let them ask two or three questions.
● When everybody has had a turn, ask the children to study their notes. Challenge them to match up people who have several things in common, pointing out that differences, too, keep friendships lively.
● Read out each pseudonym in turn, and invite the children to nominate pseudonyms that they think would make a good match, using their notes for reference.
● Ask for brief explanations why they think these two people would make good friends. Based on the children's suggestions, sort the names into pairs and write them on the board. Discretely allocate partners to any without nominations.
● Collect and return the original fact files to their owners, then encourage them to swap with their nominated friend.
● Ask each pair to role-play a telephone conversation, using each other's fact file as a springboard and stimulus. Demonstrate the difference between closed and open questions. For example, 'What colour belt are you working for in Judo?' (closed); 'How difficult is it?' (open). Make sure both children have time to talk and listen.

Differentiation
Ask fluent conversationalists to role-play to the whole class as an example and discuss why their dialogue flows well. Have an adult on hand to prompt children who are struggling.

AGE RANGE 5–9

LEARNING OBJECTIVE
To share ideas to collaborate on writing a poem; to comment on and discuss each other's suggestions and assess their strengths; to use prepositions.

CURRICULUM LINKS
NLS: Y1, T1–2; Y2, T1; Y3, T1–3; Y4, T1 & T3; Y5, T3.

My amazing journey

What you need
The 'My amazing journey' photocopiable sheet on page 48; whiteboard; marker pens.

What to do
● Make one enlarged copy of the photocopiable sheet.
● Tell the children that they are going on a journey. It will be an amazing journey, as they won't be travelling except in their imaginations.
● Explain that they will need to use prepositions; words that tell us where we are in relation to something else. Offer some suggestions, for example, 'The wall is behind you'; 'Where is the ceiling?' 'Above us'. Demonstrate that different prepositions are suited to different situations: 'If there was a tunnel, would we go round, through or along it?'

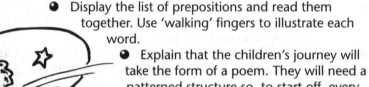

● Display the list of prepositions and read them together. Use 'walking' fingers to illustrate each word.
● Explain that the children's journey will take the form of a poem. They will need a patterned structure so, to start off, every line will begin with a preposition. Invite suggestions as to which preposition to 'set off' with, followed by an appropriate location, for example, 'Under... the bridge'; '... the trees' and so on. Discuss the suggestions, choosing the one that offers the most creative potential.
● Now ask for adjectives to describe, for example, the bridge. Introduce alliterative words such as big; brick; beautiful; bouncy; brittle. Discuss which two adjectives work well together to paint a picture in words, then write the chosen line on the board.
● Pick another preposition, new location and alliterative adjectives. Write the new line below the first and read them aloud to check for a pleasing rhythm, sound and sense. Add a third line, similarly constructed. Avoid using the same prepositions or adjectives.
● For the fourth line choose a suitable verb, based on the journey locations so far, for example, 'we crept; tiptoed; hurried'. Inset this line slightly, to give the poem shape and indicate a change of pace.
● For an optional fifth line, introduce repetition by repeating line four but this time substituting an adverb in place of the personal pro-noun. The first stanza might look something like this: (Beginning each line with a capital is traditional, but optional):

Under the beautiful, brick bridge,
Along the pink, pebbly path,
Through the terrible, twisty tunnel,
    We crawled,
    Carefully crawled.

● Reread the stanza together, then carry on with your poem.

Differentiation
Supply insecure writers with the layout, prepositions in place, for them to continue. Allow children to write another stanza. Challenge them to think of a surprise ending.

AGE RANGE 8–11

LEARNING OBJECTIVE
To generate ideas for a collaborative poem; to listen to each other's suggestions, comment and develop ideas using rhythm, rhyme and alliteration.

CURRICULUM LINKS
NLS: Y4, T1–3; Y5, T1; Y6, T3.

Down our sofa

What you need
Whiteboard; marker pens.

What to do
● Play a game with the children. Tell them to be brave; they are going to put their hand down the back of a very, very old sofa! Explain that it has been in the family for generations, and briefly discuss its condition (lumpy; broken springs; covered in cat hairs and so on).

● Demonstrate putting your hand down the back of the pretend sofa. Explain that there is grit under your nails. Where could it have come from? Perhaps a flower-pot? Or a biscuit? Act holding half a biscuit. What sort is it? How long has it been there?

● Invite individuals to put their hand down the back of the sofa and see what they find. Keep ideas plausible but encourage children to elaborate, by example and invitation. For example, they found… a lollipop. What flavour? Whose was it? What's stuck to it? Ugh! Fluff? Hairs? Dog-hairs? What colour?

● Ask what is wrong with things, for example, a pencil; is it broken? A doll; where are its arms? Continue developing tactile ideas, using all of the senses and increasing detail.

● Demonstrate how to draft the ideas into a descriptive list poem, using rhyming couplets. Collect rhymes and eliminate useless ones to show how rhymes should not appear forced and must be subservient to meaning. For example:

A sharp white shard from a chipped china plate
A King George florin…

● Break off to collect '-ate' rhymes (including variant spellings). Eliminate unsuitable words, for example, 'A King George florin that's just light-weight' makes only grammatical sense and sounds terribly forced.

● Having eliminated such words, ask for suggestions using a suitable rhyme, for example, 'A King George florin dated nineteen-forty-eight'. Draw attention to opportunities to use alliteration, such as the repeated 'f' in 'florin' and 'forty' makes this a more assonant choice than, say, 'thirty-eight'.

● Stress that poetry is an oral art. As the poem develops, keep reading it aloud together to listen for pleasing sounds and rhythm, checking sense. Adjust the rhythm by using abbreviations to lose a syllable or longer words to gain syllables, explaining that this is part of the drafting process. Ask the children to listen to each others' suggestions and discuss choices.

● Introduce a chorus, to avoid monotony. You could draw on the sofa's attributes, insetting it as you write, for example:

Sinking sofa
Spongy, smelly sofa
Who knows what we'll find!

Differentiation
Collect a few small items as a starting point for less imaginative children to observe and handle. Encourage able children to make up further stanzas by themselves.

AGE RANGE 5–11

LEARNING OBJECTIVE
To recognise and use questions; to listen to others and respond appropriately; to use inferentially logical thought processes.

CURRICULUM LINKS
NLS: Y1, T3; Y2, T3; Y4, T1; Y5, T1; Y6, T1–2.

Fox and rabbits

What you need
A chair for each child.

What to do
● Arrange chairs in a circle. Invite the children to sit down, explaining that they are 'rabbits'.
● Take on the role of 'fox', standing in the centre of the circle.
● Ask a closed question, such as: 'Is your birthday in July?' Explain that any child who answers 'yes' must get up from their chair, or 'rabbit hole', and hurry to occupy another free chair. Practise this with a few different questions until the children are familiar with the idea.
● Remove one chair and ask its occupant to join you in the circle as 'fox'. Let the child ask a practice question and wait for the rabbits to respond.
● Before asking the fox to pose a second new question, explain that, this time, the fox will try to seat him or herself on an empty chair (dive down a rabbit hole) before it becomes reoccupied. If successful, they become a rabbit again and the child left without a seat becomes the new fox.
● As the children become familiar with the game, ask for their opinions on good questions and bad questions. For example, some questions will require honesty and good memory on the part of the participants: 'Did you have an egg for breakfast?'; while some may be self-evident: 'Are you wearing long sleeves?'
● Discuss how they can use strategy in their questions; if the foxes have some idea which rabbits will have to move, they can be ready to hurry to a vacant seat. They might, for example, spot some stained fingers so they could ask: 'Who did painting after lunch?'
● Encourage a variety of question styles and subject matter including predictable, visual-clue questions and honesty-reliant, unobvious questions.
● Discourage judgemental questions of a personal nature, such as 'anyone with messy hair' or 'anyone in a bad mood' or questions to which children can adjust their behaviour and cause chaos, such as 'anyone smiling'.

Differentiation
Give time for younger children to prepare and rehearse a few questions beforehand. Challenge older or more able foxes to ask a question that will receive a positive response from only one or a small specified number of children, requiring an elimination approach to thinking. For example, they could work out that only one child in the class has a name beginning with a chosen letter.

Speaking and
Listening Games

AGE RANGE 7–11

LEARNING OBJECTIVE
To listen attentively and discuss a poem, its effectiveness and use of language, expressing agreement or disagreement; to generate ideas for own writing.

CURRICULUM LINKS
NLS: Y2, T1–2; Y3, T1; Y4, T2; Y5, T2; Y6, T3.

Just one wish

What you need
The 'Just one wish' photocopiable sheet on page 49; paper; pencils.

What to do
● Make one copy of the photocopiable sheet for each child.
● Ask the children, if they had only one wish, what would they wish for? Encourage them to elaborate and explain their answers. Note which are for concrete things and which for abstract things, drawing attention to the distinction between the two. If children wish for broad abstracts such as 'happiness', ask for an example of how others could tell they were happy if their wish were granted; how would happiness manifest itself?
● Give each child a copy of the poem and read it aloud to the children as they follow the words.
● When you have finished reading, ask the children to think about how the poet felt when she wrote the poem. What images has she used to convey a feeling of happiness? (The subtitle of the original poem reads 'feeling full of joy'.)
● Point out that none of the wishes in the poem is concrete; all are abstract.
● Reflect on the verbs used in the second line of the first four verses. These are far from abstract: drip, throw, plant, burn.
● Which senses does the poem involve? Ask the children to support their answers with examples from the text.
● Consider the format of the poem. What is the same about every stanza? (First lines; number of lines; rhythm; voice). Which senses does the poet not involve?
● How does the last stanza differ? Is the poet inviting us to look again at nature and natural phenomena with the same wonder as the first time we saw it?
● Working individually or in pairs, ask the children to write a new verse for the poem. They must retain the format of the other verses and involve one or more senses, if possible including sound or taste.
● Challenge them to find an evocative verb for the second line, for example, if their wish is to 'smell' something they might 'breathe' or 'absorb'.

Differentiation
If children find it difficult to think in abstracts, encourage them to think of a concrete object and replace it with the word 'wish'. For example, if they wished for a bicycle, they might 'ride it' and develop a listening concept from its associated bell: 'If I had only one wish / I would ride it downhill, free-wheeling to the voice of bells…'.

AGE RANGE 5–10

LEARNING OBJECTIVE
To listen attentively to others' accounts and ask pertinent questions; to write descriptively.

CURRICULUM LINKS
NLS: Y1, T1–3; Y2, T1–3; Y3, T1; Y4, T1; Y5, T1.

Here is a place

What you need
Brief preparation of descriptive facts about a place that you know well and feel strongly about, either for positive or negative reasons; thesauruses.

What to do
● Tell the children about a place that you know very well. Explain that you would like to show them a picture but you don't have one. Instead you are going to describe it, painting a picture in words.
● Do so, drawing especially on your feelings and involving your senses, for example, 'When you arrive, you feel …'; 'After a while, you hear …'; 'Sometimes there's the smell of …', and so on.
● Ask the children if it sounds like a place that they would like to go to. If so, why? If not, what put them off? Can they tell whether you love or loathe the place? How? Examine the language devices that you used to paint a graphic picture and sustain their interest, such as talking about colours or using similes, for example, 'The grass brushed my face and felt like a butterfly's wing.'
● Ask the children to close their eyes and think of a place that they love or loathe. This might be a holiday destination or a theme park they visited, or simply a favourite armchair or a warm bubble bath. Encourage a specific place, for example, 'on the swing where my toes touch the hollihocks', rather than broadly 'in a garden'.
● Encourage the children to look around at what they can see in their mind's eye. What can they smell? Taste? Hear? Touch?
● Organise the children into groups of two or three. Explain that one must describe their special place while their partners listen carefully and ask questions. Remind the speakers to try to create a strong sense of place and atmosphere to evoke feelings in their listeners, similar to their own. After a short while, and on your given signal, speakers should change over.
● Regroup and talk about the activity. Did children feel as if they had almost been there when they heard their partner's description? Could they all tell whether the speaker loved or loathed the place? How?
● Having voiced their feelings about their chosen place, ask the children to draft a poem about it. Use the feedback from the partners in each group to discover which descriptions were most vivid.
● Hear the early drafts and invite constructive criticism.
● Encourage the children to give their poems titles.

Differentiation
Suggest that insecure writers use a pattern, beginning each verse, 'Here is a place, where…'. For more confident writers, encourage redrafting of poems to strengthen their impact, for example, using thesauruses to find more evocative adjectives.

Speaking and
Listening Games

BRIGHT
IDEAS

Translators

●   Join the speech bubbles which are saying the same thing, but in different words:

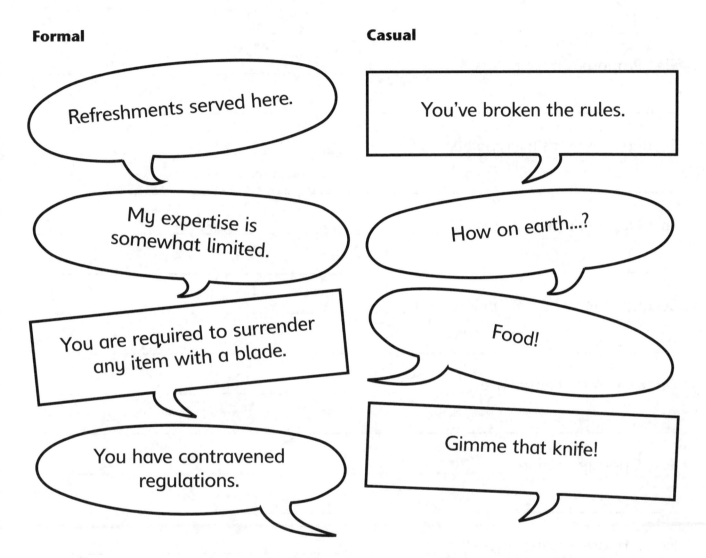

Formal   **Casual**

Refreshments served here.

You've broken the rules.

My expertise is somewhat limited.

How on earth...?

You are required to surrender any item with a blade.

Food!

You have contravened regulations.

Gimme that knife!

●   Can you translate these speech bubbles? Use a dictionary or thesaurus to help you. Write in the thought-bubble, in simple terms, what you think they are saying.

I hold you in high esteem.

Please reconcile your differences.

Alert our reception on your arrival.

Pros and cons

Debate proposal: This house believes (ie 'We think…') _____

_____

First Proposer's main points: _____

_____

Second Proposer's main points: _____

_____

First Opposer's main points: _____

_____

Second Opposer's main points: _____

_____

Floor Speaker's comments: _____

_____

First Opposer's summary: _____

_____

First Proposer's summary: _____

_____

Chairman's closing remarks, before voting and result announcement: _____

_____

**Speaking and
Listening Games**

Guess who?

Horse rider
Joust glider
Music maker
Floor shaker
Tennis prancer
Heavy dancer
Diet hater
Serial dater
Dandy dresser
Wife stresser
Church leader
Poor breeder
Nifty speaker
Divorce seeker
Armour filler
Wife killer
Monk basher
Law smasher
Banquet boozer
Bad loser.

© Coral Rumble

Picture it

Princess Polly

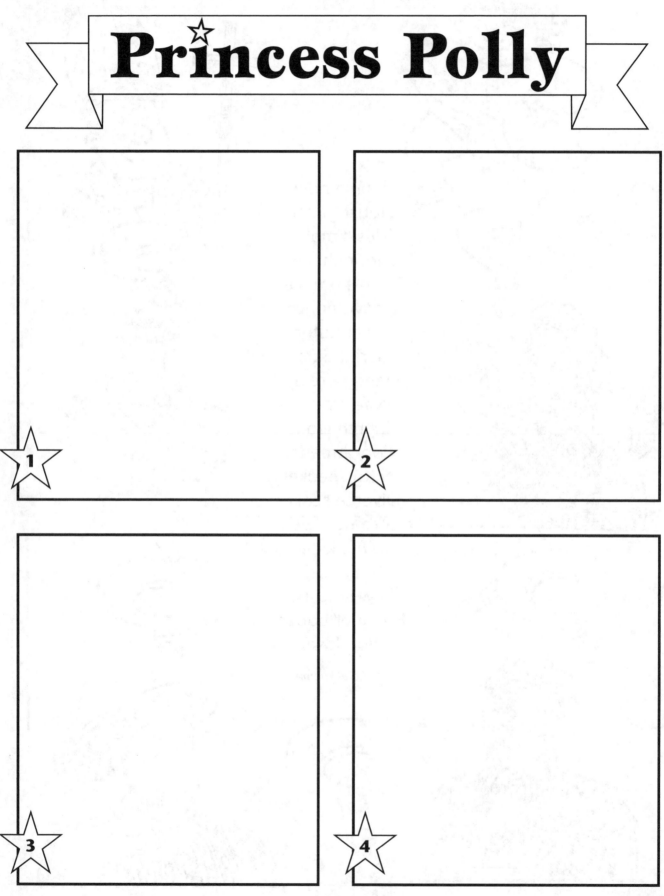

1

2

3

4

Speaking and
Listening Games

Two's company

Fact file

Pseudonym (a made-up name) _____

Age _____

What I look like: _____

Height _____ Other features _____

Interests:
Indoors_____ Outdoors _____

Favourites:
Music _____ Animal _____

Hobby _____ Holiday destination_____

Game _____ TV programme _____

Clothes_____ School activity_____

When I grow up I'd like to be _____

What annoys me most in other people is _____

What I like best in other people is_____

I like collecting _____

On Saturdays I like to _____

Personality (circle those that apply to you):

easygoing / strong sense of humour / worrier / pernickety
untidy / neat / serious / brave / funny / sporty / friendly / shy
talkative / lazy / active / theatrical / thoughtful / kind
always in a hurry / slow / careless / careful

My amazing journey

into	above
out of	towards
through	after
below	inside
around	beneath
down	over
up	along
behind	past
under	between

Speaking and
Listening Games

Just one wish

If I had only one wish
I would drip it in a rippling pool
and watch the concentric circles
it would make as it plunged downwards
fragmenting the surface of the water.

If I had only one wish
I'd throw it high into the blue heaven
and watch is as it arched over
and tumbled down, creating
a rainbow of joy in the roof of the world.

If I had only one wish
I'd plant it deep in brown earth
and watch as it pierced the loam
with a pointed spear
and grew into a magnificent tree.

If I had only one wish
I'd burn it like incense
and savour the aroma as it wafted
far away on the winds of perfume
and dissipated on the thermals of life.

If I had only one wish
I should wish that everyone
could again be filled with childlike joy
so that the magic and beauty of the world
would once again be a daily miracle.

© Janis Priestley

CHAPTER 3

Group discussion

AGE RANGE 5–8

LEARNING OBJECTIVE
To take turns to speak and listen, sharing ideas; to define criteria to make a decision and present findings to the rest of the class.

CURRICULUM LINKS
NLS: Y1, T2; Y2, T3; Y3, T1.

On the board

What you need
A display area; whiteboard and pens; paper; pencils.

What to do
● Draw the children's attention to current displays in the classroom. Look at the purpose behind them. Are they decorative, informative or both? Is the function of each the same? Do some pay tribute to good work? Discuss which displays are most eye-catching and why. Consider ways in which they could be improved, perhaps by using different materials or colour-schemes. Would ribbons or balloons attract the eye or detract from the purpose?

● If possible, take the children on a walk around the school to look at displays in the hall or corridors. Point out any thematic approaches, such as a border of sandcastles around a display of seaside poems.

● Indicate the available display area in the classroom, and point out the potential for exhibiting work, highlighting topics, sharing information and so on.

● Explain that you are going to allocate this display area to the children's own choice of display. For a limited period, they may decide on its content. It might be their own art gallery, a class news board or perhaps anonymous baby photographs from home to create a match-the-face game. Ask them to consider how they can make best use of the space.

● Divide the children into groups. Explain that you would like them to discuss ideas for using the display area, and decide which suggestion to present to the rest of the class, after considering its format in greater detail. One or two children from each group should present their choice, giving reasons for their idea.

● Agree on a shorthand title that sums up each suggestion, such as 'Quizzes and puzzles' or 'Hobbies', and write all of the ideas on the board. Invite a whole-class debate on each idea in turn, encouraging the children to ask questions about each proposal.

● Take a vote on each suggestion before announcing the most popular choice. Ask the groups to reform and discuss how the space might look, drawing a plan of their ideas.

● Decide on elements from each group's plans, for example, a border from one group, a style of heading from another, then work together to create your display.

Differentiation
Write discussion areas, such as colour scheme, materials and content, on the board to facilitate dialogue between younger children. Older children could produce a scale-drawing of the area, combining 2-D and 3-D aspects. Help children to write captions for the display.

AGE RANGE 8–11

LEARNING OBJECTIVE
To investigate and reflect on beliefs and discuss motivations behind rational and irrational behaviour.

CURRICULUM LINKS
NLS: Y4, T1; Y6, T1.

Cause and effect?

What you need
The 'Cause and effect' photocopiable sheet on page 66; pencils.

What to do
● Make one copy of the photocopiable sheet for each child.
● Tell the children that, when you get home, you are going to thoroughly relax. Ask if they believe you. Some may, some may not, but all being well, you do expect to relax.
● Ask, if you had made the same statement and touched wood, would it be more or less likely to happen? Are the children's answers based on fact or belief? Avoid being judgemental, but encourage discussion on the rationale behind their responses.
● Explain that superstitions are as old as the world. At an early age we recognise cause and effect. If we bump our head, it hurts. If we smile, people smile back. Inevitably, sometimes, we make false connections, mistakenly attributing one event to being a consequence of another. Read the following widespread superstitions:

> See a penny; pick it up; all day long you'll have good luck.
> It is a good omen if a black cat crosses your path.
> If you break a mirror, you will have seven years' bad luck.
> It is bad luck to walk under a ladder.
> It is unlucky to open an umbrella indoors.
> Spilled salt is unlucky unless you throw some of the spilt grains over your left shoulder, then you will be safe.

● Do any of these statements offer good advice? Is it really 'luck' or common sense? For example, an umbrella in a confined space might poke someone's eye or break valuable ornaments. What sort of bad luck could you experience if you walked under a ladder?
● Point out that, whether we believe superstitions or not, we should recognise that they are based on opinions or fears rather than fact. Different cultures have different superstitions. None is more right or wrong, more reasonable or unreasonable, than any other.
● Propose that it is human nature to look for cause and effect, whether valid or not.
● In groups, discuss superstitions that the children have heard of or practise and any that they remember believing, but have now outgrown.
● Give each child a photocopiable sheet to complete. Encourage them to think up ideas that have their roots in a possible 'cause and effect' scenario.

Differentiation
Write common examples of superstitions on the board to help younger children. For older children, erase the nouns in the example and ask them to substitute others.

BRIGHT IDEAS Speaking and Listening Games

AGE RANGE 9–11

LEARNING OBJECTIVE
To make notes when listening ready to plan a group interpretation; to listen to suggestions, agree on preferences and allocate actions.

CURRICULUM LINKS
NLS: Y5, T1; Y6, T3.

Red arrows

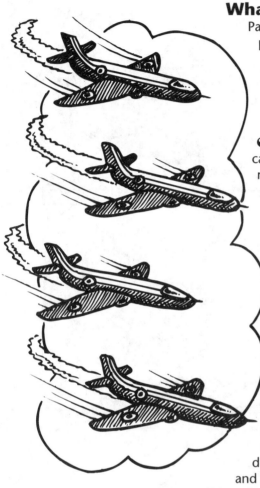

What you need
Paper; pencils; the 'Red Arrows' photocopiable sheet on page 67; an action photograph of a Red Arrows air display (optional); safe, open space (indoors or outside).

What to do
● Ask the children to listen carefully while you read the article about the Red Arrows.
● When you have finished reading, ask whether anyone can remember any of the verbs describing the aircraft movements?
● Give each child a piece of paper and a pencil. Explain that you are going to re-read the article and, this time, you would like the children to take notes.
● When you have finished reading, ask the children to tell you some of the verbs that they wrote down, such as 'whoosh', 'zoom', 'weave', 'spiral', 'plummet', 'climb', 'spin' and 'twist'. What do the verbs have in common? (All involve movement.) Which verbs gave them a strong mental picture of the kite-like effect? Does anyone think they can draw a diagram to show how the aircraft would be lined up?
● Divide the children into groups of six. Ask one group to arrange themselves into a triangle. Explain that they are a Red Arrowheads (or Triangles!) Display Team. In this formation, each group must plan a sequence of movements to perform a synchronised display. They may separate from their triangle formation and re-form, as the Red Arrows Air Display teams do. Although they will be on the ground, not in the air, they must choose movements to reflect the verbs used in the article.
● Encourage the children to make good use of height, space, speed, stretching and bending and taking weight on different parts of their body. For example, a sequence might include a forward roll.
● When each group has agreed on a sequence they must learn it and practise performing 'as one'. Invite the groups to spread out and make use of the space as they develop and discuss practical ideas. Encourage children to move smoothly from one action to the next.
● Allow some time for the children to practise, then bring the whole class together to give their performances in turn. Invite comments on each group's finished displays. Encourage the children to share their tips for synchronising, such as carefully watching each other; counting; following the leader; using an outstretched arm as a measure and so on.

Differentiation
Provide copies of the article for children to follow as you read. Encourage younger children to underline the verbs, then help them to interpret each into a movement. Ask more confident children to practise interpreting the verbs individually before working together. Build up to a group of six from working in with one partner.

AGE RANGE 7–11

LEARNING OBJECTIVE
To plan and discuss, making sure that all group members help implement ideas after reaching agreement.

CURRICULUM LINKS
NLS: Y3, T2; Y4, T1–2; Y5, T1; Y6, T3.

Tabletop game

What you need
Pencils; crayons; paper; dice; the 'Tabletop game' photocopiable sheet on page 68; card.

What to do
● Make one enlarged copy of the photocopiable sheet on card for each group.
● Tell the children they are going to work in groups to devise a tabletop board game. The game will involve moving counters on the throw of dice, but they must add other elements. Briefly consider aspects of, for example, 'Snakes and Ladders' and 'Monopoly'. Both are counter and dice games, but each has different elements, including bonuses and hazards.
● Show the children the basic tabletop game sheet and discuss how they can use the layout. For example, they might decide that squares adopt some significance over circles, or that coloured circles represent forfeits or bonuses such as 'miss a turn' or 'have another go'.
● Explain that each group will need to give its game a setting and a motive, such as traversing the jungle to reach a village, avoiding wild animals and booby traps along the way. They must devise rules, forfeits and bonuses, plan the board and design thematic, distinctive counters.
● Point out potential pitfalls, such as a bonus square leading to a forfeit square creating a loop that becomes an impasse. Any hazards or bonuses should be thematic. For example, a hazard in an undersea-themed game might be 'Meet a shark; miss a turn'.
● Encourage the children to add extras to their board, such as instruction cards to pick up, or short cut spaces. Advise them to draft their ideas in pencil and try them out before designing the game in full colour. Check for flaws and for a balance of good and bad spaces.
● Advise the children to allocate tasks within their group, then give them plenty of time to work on their games.
● When everyone has finished, invite the groups to swap game boards. Ask the children to play each other's games and offer feedback on the clarity of the rules and success and enjoyment of the game. Have they said who starts? If two dice are used, what happens if a double is thrown? Do you need to throw a 6 to start or shake an exact number to finish? Are the written instructions legible?

Differentiation
Add numbers and direction arrows to the trail for younger children. Let older children devise their games-boards from scratch, including the layout.

AGE RANGE 9–11

LEARNING OBJECTIVE
To research in groups and present findings to the class.

CURRICULUM LINKS
NLS: Y5, T1-2; Y6, T3.

Who, what, when, where?

What you need
Historical resources; historical books with reference to inventions, famous people, arts and science; access to the Internet; classical music from different periods; music from the 20th century; music-playing facilities.

What to do
● Explain the different meanings of the word 'contemporary'. Tell the children that it can mean within our time but, in an historical context, it means within the same time as someone or something else of that period.
● Invite the children to work in groups to conduct some historical research. Explain that each group will choose a famous event or invention, and this will form the springboard of their research. Tell them that they will be finding information, not only about the event or invention, but also about contemporary life, so that they can place the event or invention in its historical setting. Once they have gathered their information, they are going to present their findings to the class in an interesting way.
● Let the children have free access to the resources, books and Internet. As the group members collect information, encourage them to disseminate it to other groups under headings such as 'art', 'music', 'costume', 'literature', 'houses' and 'home'. For example, which musicians were composing at the time when Alexander Bell was inventing the telephone? What sort of entertainment did families enjoy? Find examples of poems and novels, art and sculpture from the period. What were clothes and houses like? Encourage the children to move into research groups within their chosen field and then return to their original groups to plan their presentation.
● Allow time for the children to plan their presentation. This might include playing sample music or having an art reproduction on hand as a visual aid. They might choose to create simple costume props such as models or drawings to support their presentations.
● Plan to spread the presentations over several sessions, depending on the depth of research. Alternatively, ask the children to present simple five-minute 'tasters' of the period.

Differentiation
Support younger children in finding their information. Direct them to relevant websites or sections in the books. Older children could go into character to present their findings, wearing costumes and using props to support their presentations.

AGE RANGE 8–11

LEARNING OBJECTIVE
To share and explain views and decide on the most effective way of relaying findings to the rest of the class.

CURRICULUM LINKS
NLS: Y4, T2–3; Y5, T1 & T3; Y6, T2.

National 'You decide' Day

What you need
Paper; pencils; art materials.

What to do
● Talk about National Days with the children. Invite the children to offer their own thoughts about the purposes and advantages of such days. Explain that some, such as Poppy Day, are commemorative, while others, such as National Stop Smoking Day, are dedicated to issues that people want to highlight for the greater good of society.
● In groups, ask the children to think about and discuss a cause that they think deserves a dedicated National Day. Once they have chosen a cause or issue, the group should decide how they will present their ideas to the rest of the class. Their presentation might involve a mini-drama, a poster campaign or perhaps a letter addressed to schools and other institutions and organisations seeking support. They should aim to inform the class of the reason behind their choice and the benefits that they hope would stem from it.
● To accompany their presentation, invite each group to design and produce prototypes of posters advertising the day, and badges or emblems for supporters to wear. These materials should highlight the rationale behind the group's choice.
● Give each group sufficient time to give their presentations, then talk about ways in which you can measure the success of the presentation. For instance, has anyone changed their views on a particular subject? Could they recruit more volunteers to the cause? What do they think would justify their National Day becoming an annual occasion?

Differentiation
Begin with a whole-class discussion and choice of National Day, dividing into groups only to discuss the details of design and format of the day and its paraphernalia. Allocate roles, such as campaign recruiter or spokesperson, to more confident children.

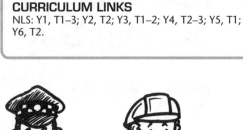

AGE RANGE 5–11

LEARNING OBJECTIVE
To offer ideas and information; to ask and answer
questions to plan a whole-class presentation; to take
brief notes.

CURRICULUM LINKS
NLS: Y1, T1–3; Y2, T2; Y3, T1–2; Y4, T2–3; Y5, T1;
Y6, T2.

Because you're worth it!

What you need

Whiteboard; marker pens; paper; pencils; poetry and song books.

What to do

● Gather the children together and initiate a discussion about people who help us. Invite suggestions from the children about helpers in the school and the wider community, for example, the school cook, lunchtime supervisors, police, crossing patrol people, parent helpers, nurse, librarian and so on.

● Explain that some of these jobs are paid and some are voluntary, but all contribute to everyone's well-being. Pose a question to the children: if they had the opportunity to say a special 'thank you' to one person or a group of people, who would it be and why? Take suggestions and hold a whole-class discussion of their merits.

● Talk about special celebration days such as Mother's Day, when people have the opportunity to show their appreciation and say 'thank you'.

● Organise the children into groups and provide them with writing materials. In each group, appoint roles such as scribe and spokesperson.

● In their groups, ask the children to think about a person that helps them and discuss ways in which they can show their appreciation of that person. In simplest form, they could make, sign and deliver a card. In grander form, they might plan a variety performance with music, poetry, speeches and thematic PE and dance displays, in their chosen person's honour. Encourage the children who are scribes to use abbreviations and key words in their notes.

● Listen to embryo ideas via each group's spokesperson and invite comments from others. Ask the groups to amend their plans accordingly and begin to add detail. For example, if they decide to make a medal they should list the materials that they will need, sketch a design, decide when it will be presented and by whom. How would their chosen person be invited to the presentation ceremony?

● Bring the whole class together and ask each spokesperson to present their group's plan. Encourage other group members to help by, for example, reciting a poem or holding up a sketch to support the speaker's description.

● Take a vote on which group's plan sounds best in terms of effectiveness and realistic achievability. Briefly discuss why and ask for responses from the group as to how and why they reached their decisions.

Differentiation

Have adults act as scribes for younger children. With older children, decide on broad ideas as a whole-class discussion, then delegate areas such as 'choose a poem', 'write a speech' or 'design a card' to different groups.

AGE RANGE 7–11

LEARNING OBJECTIVE
To adopt the roles of leader, scribe, mentor and reporter; to create a set of rules.

CURRICULUM LINKS
NLS: Y3, T2–3; Y4, T3; Y5, T1 & T3; Y6, T2.

Classroom clutter

What you need
Paper; pencils; flip chart; pens.

What to do
● Talk to the children about their classroom environment. Ask them to say what they like about their classroom, from the colour of the walls to the arrangement of tables. Point out how the cleaners help to maintain its cleanliness and appearance. Recognise, too, how examples of their efforts displayed on walls, add to the positive atmosphere of the classroom.

● Explain that if we are untidy or disorganised no cleaners in the world can make the room a pleasant place in which to work and learn. It may well be that you already have classroom rules in place relating to tidiness, use of bins, disposal of recyclable waste and so on, but perhaps they may be improved.

● Organise the children into teams. Ask each team to invent an imaginative name for their group to suggest that they represent a 'Tidy Team'. Encourage each team to devise their ideal tidiness policy for the classroom, bearing in mind that their targets should be practical, easily managed and fair to all.

● To facilitate the sharing of ideas, ask each team to appoint a leader to chair their discussion and ensure that everyone's opinion is heard, a scribe to take accurate notes, a mentor to seek clarification of any suggestions, and a reporter to deliver their suggestions to the rest of the class.

● Ask the children to consider whether a tidy classroom is, in itself, sufficient motivation or whether there should be incentives or rewards for the tidiest team?

● Invite reporters to present their team's ideas to the whole class. Scribes may assist the reporter's presentation by writing bullet-points or drawing diagrams on the flip-chart. Invite constructive feedback from others.

● As a class, decide on which of the suggestions to adopt. Draw up a rota for implementing the chosen policies.

Differentiation
Assign a limited area of classroom care to each group, such as paper storage, art materials and topic tables. Older children could consider areas beyond their classroom, such as the corridors, cloakroom and playground.

AGE RANGE 5–8

LEARNING OBJECTIVE
To take turns to contribute and justify ideas; to use commas to separate items in a list.

CURRICULUM LINKS
NLS: Y1, T1–2; Y2, T2; Y3, T1

Have you packed?

What you need
The 'Have you packed?' photocopiable sheet on page 69; pencils; whiteboard; pens.

What to do
● Make one copy of the photocopiable sheet for each child.
● Invite the children to imagine that they are going on holiday. They can pack one suitcase, but it cannot contain any clothes – they are 'already packed'!
● Hold up a photocopiable sheet. Show the children that a teddy, toothbrush and toothpaste are 'already packed', and draw their attention to the three words in the list on the suitcase lid.
● Give each child a game sheet then organise the children into groups.
● Appoint a spokesperson for each group. Explain that the spokesperson is going to keep a master sheet for their group, and ask them to wait a few minutes while the rest of the group 'packs their suitcases'.
● Allow a few minutes for each child to 'pack their suitcase', drawing pictures in the case and adding the names of the items to the list on the suitcase lid, separated by commas. Limited space in the suitcase means that they must have a good reason for choosing anything they take.
● To begin with, children compete within their groups taking turns to ask: 'Have you packed… (item)?', adding the name of an item from their own list. They, and anyone else who has packed it, can add one tally mark to their sheet. The spokesperson then draws the picture and adds the name of the item to their 'master sheet'.
● Play continues, moving clockwise around the group. As the spokesperson's suitcase starts to become full, anyone in the group may challenge an item for its packer to justify. If everyone agrees, then the item stays in the master suitcase and scores a point for the packer. Otherwise it is 'left at home' and the packer loses a point from their individual sheet. The aim is to pack as much as possible.
● When each master suitcase is full, individual scores can be added up. Then ask the spokespeople to add their group's combined score.
● Taking the top scorers first, ask each spokesperson to read their master sheet list. Any item that is unique to any one group scores another tally mark for that group. The group with the highest overall score wins.

Differentiation
Let younger children just draw the items in their suitcase. For more able children, modify the game using other scenarios, such as food for a party. Challenge the children to set their own criteria to decide which should be allocated space, and which should be left behind.

58

Same poet, different poem

AGE RANGE 5–8

LEARNING OBJECTIVE
To compare two poems by the same author; to make observations and comparisons; to devise a means of ensuring all comments are voiced and discussed.

CURRICULUM LINKS
NLS: Y1, T3; Y2, T2; Y3, T1 & T3.

What you need
The 'Same poet, different poem' photocopiable sheet on page 70 (one per group); coloured crayons; paper; pencils; poetry anthologies including poems by the same poet.

What to do
● Begin by reading a few poems aloud from the poetry anthology. Talk about the words that the poets use to convey different moods, feelings and settings to the reader.

● Suggest to the children that it is very difficult to imagine summer in the middle of winter and vice versa. Through careful use of evocative language, poets can help us to imagine them.

● Tell the children that you are going to read them two poems that have been written by the same poet. Read aloud 'Summer Sun' and 'Calling, calling' by Wes Magee, from the photocopiable sheet. Establish which season is being described in each poem. Tell the children that you are going to give them copies of the poems to reread and compare.

● Appoint a leader to head each group's discussion and make sure that everyone can have their say. It might be helpful to appoint a mentor to each group to help clarify any comments, a scribe to take notes and a spokesperson to share the group's findings with the rest of the class.

● During their discussion, the children should decide what they like about the poems and why. Consider the use of words and the pattern of each poem. Circulate among the groups, prompting discussion by asking questions. Which words in the poems add atmosphere and the feeling of the season? (The warmly positive 'yes'; the evocatively cold 'grey'.) What poetic devices can they find? (Rhyme, repetition, alliteration.) What are the rhyme patterns? Poem shapes? Compare subject matter and number of verses. What effect do the repeated 's' sounds have? Are they relaxing? sleepy? Consider the onomatopoeic effect of the stuttering start to 'stalling' in 'Calling, calling', and the similes in 'Summer Sun'.

● Bring the children together again. Invite individuals or pairs to read or recite each poem aloud, then invite the children to discuss their findings. Ask each spokesperson in turn to give a broad statement on their group's feelings about the poems. Ask questions to encourage them to reveal the results of their discussion. What was it about the poem that made you feel warm and relaxed? Which verbs made you strongly visualise playing in the snow? Do other groups agree or have additional comments? Did either poem make them appreciate either season more than they did before?

Differentiation
Supply different coloured crayons and encourage younger children to underline rhymes, highlight alliteration, ring verbs and so on. Encourage older children to find more poems by the same poet.

AGE RANGE 8–11

LEARNING OBJECTIVE
To compare two poems by the same author and make observations; to devise strategies to ensure all members' comments are voiced and discussed.

CURRICULUM LINKS
NLS: Y4, T1–3; Y5, T3; Y6, T2–3.

Compare and contrast

What you need
The 'Compare and contrast' photocopiable sheet on page 71 (one between each pair of children); coloured crayons; paper; pencils; poetry anthologies including poems by the same poet.

What to do
● Distribute one photocopiable sheet between each pair of children. Point out that both poems are written by the same poet, Jill Townsend. Ask the children to read the poems together. Decide what they are about. Who are the speakers? Neither is a conventional poem with stanzas, yet both are poems. Briefly discuss how they can tell. Can they identify any poetic devices?
● Amalgamate pairs to form groups of six children. Choose one child from each group to read the poems aloud to the others and act as spokesperson. Discuss delivery and emphasis, thinking about where to pause and change pace in the reading. Encourage the children to experiment with their voice and phrasing to retain the sense while recognising the rhythm of the poems.
● Ask the children to discuss the form and content of each poem. How do the poems make them feel? Amused? Sad? Why? What do the poems have in common? They are both written in the first person, they both have historical background, both involve mishaps; one deliberate to make a point, the other alluding to an impending disaster, one speaks with the benefit of amused wisdom and the other in poignant ignorance.

● Let the children share their observations. Invite readers to perform the poems before beginning your discussion. Ask questions to encourage feedback. How does the poet evoke emotion through her use of language? How does the informal language used in 'Canute's Account' contrast with the old-fashioned, formal language in 'Letter to My Uncle'? Consider the irony in each poem. Compare the contrasting pace of the poems.
● Examine the effects of assonance in 'Letter to My Uncle'. Discuss the repeated vowel sounds, such as the short 'i' in 'biggest thing afloat' and the long 'oo', in 'too cruel'. Consider how this slows the pace of the poem to emphasise first the boy's wonder and second his imagined frustration at being denied permission.
● Ask the children to sum up why each poem works so well.

Differentiation
Supply different coloured crayons for so that younger children can underline rhymes, highlight assonance and so on. Encourage older children to find more poems by the same poet.

AGE RANGE 9–11

LEARNING OBJECTIVE
To share opinions to form a consensus; to understand the concept of mythical creatures and create such fictional characters.

CURRICULUM LINKS
NLS: Y5, T1; Y6, T1.

Myth and material

What you need
An enlarged copy of the 'Myth and material' photocopiable sheet on page 72 for each group of five or six children; pencils; whiteboard; pens.

What to do
● Explore the notion that we seem to know about things that we have not only never seen, but that do not exist. Ask for a volunteer to describe a mermaid. Does everybody agree with the description? How do they actually know what a mermaid looks like, when they have never seen one?
● Explain that broad, universal agreement is called a consensus. In this instance we arrive at it through generations of folk-legend.
● Divide the class into groups, assigning the role of scribe to one member in each. Give one photocopiable sheet to each group. Ask the children to discuss what they 'know' about dragons, and the scribes to fill in the spider diagram on the sheet using single words or short phrases such as 'breathes fire', 'has a pointed tail', 'lives in a cave' and 'guards treasure'.
● Encourage the children to appoint a spokesperson in each group to voice their findings.
Ask questions to get the discussion started, for example, 'What does your dragon eat?' Check whether other groups agree.
● Open up any disagreements to discussion. For example, a dragon in Wales might be red (as on the flag) whereas other dragons might be green or brown, like a reptile. Explain that slight variation is valid within a consensus.
● Next, encourage the children to choose one of the materials on their photocopiable sheet. Brainstorm its properties and connotations to produce a similarly broad spider diagram about things that they know about that material. For example, if they chose 'paper', they could add arrows leading to the words and phrases: 'fragile'; 'tears easily'; 'absorbs water'; 'used to make decorations'; 'printed on'; 'made into books'; 'can be thin, like tissue or thick, like card' and so on.
● Ask the children to develop a fictional character, mixing the dragon characteristics with the material properties. For example, they might think of a paper dragon that breathes confetti and guards a paper recycling plant.
● Invite the children to draw pictures of their character and write its characteristics underneath.

Differentiation
Ask younger children direct questions: What does it eat? Where does it live? Encourage groups of older children to develop a story plot around their character.

AGE RANGE 8–11

LEARNING OBJECTIVE
To take on different roles within a group.

CURRICULUM LINKS
NLS: Y4, T2–3; Y5, T1 & T3; Y6, T2.

Looking for a job?

What you need
Pencils; paper; whiteboard; pens.

What to do:
● On the board write the following:

ADVERTISEMENT: Reliable boy or girl wanted as Class Representative on the School Council. Applicants should be articulate and willing to represent others' views whether or not they are in agreement. An ability to present a rational, concise report on school matters is essential. If you have enthusiasm, commitment to your fellow classmates and a little spare time, apply at once.

● Organise the children into groups and explain that they are interview panels. Each panel must nominate a chairperson to conduct the interview, a leader to chair the planning of the interview, a scribe to clarify the wording of questions, a mentor to clarify the purpose of questions, and a reporter to explain their final decision after the interview.
● Tell the children that they must plan an interview that will help them to appoint someone to the advertised post. Read and discuss the advertisement together. Check understanding of words such as 'articulate' and 'commitment'. Draw attention to adjectives such as 'reliable', 'willing' and 'rational'. How might they discover these qualities, or their absence, in interviewees?
● Explain that they must discuss criteria for the supposed job. What qualities would help someone to represent others responsibly? Someone who listens? Has an open mind? Is honest and approachable?
● Ask them to consider how they can help a candidate to show what they are capable of, good or bad, to help find the best person for the job. Demonstrate the limiting effect of closed questions, ('Have you been a councillor before?') compared to open questions ('Tell me about your experience as a councillor').
● Remind the children that, as they plan questions, that they should consider what they are looking for in the candidates' answers. Explain that they will need to make notes throughout to remind themselves what each candidate said in response to their questions.
● Role-play an interviewee with one group. Pretend to be suitable in some ways and not others. For example, you might be someone who speaks clearly but fidgets and doesn't listen well. Ask the panel to explain why they would or would not employ you.
● Ask two groups to work together; one as interview panel and the others role-playing diverse characters as individual applicants. Allow time for the children to conduct their interviews, then encourage the interviewers to make and explain their choice of successful candidate.

Differentiation
Provide question words and openings as starting points for less confident children. More able children could write their own job specification.

Speaking and
Listening Games

AGE RANGE 7–11

LEARNING OBJECTIVE
To use persuasive language to present a viewpoint, using a variety of oral techniques to present a convincing argument.

CURRICULUM LINKS
NLS: Y3, T1–3; Y4, T3; Y5, T3; Y6, T2.

We want a pet

What you need
Books about domestic pets and/or access to the Internet; sheets of pet-care notes (often available free from pet shops); paper; pencils.

What to do
● Arrange the class into groups, and ask each group to nominate a pet that they would like to own and look after in their own home.
● Encourage the groups to organise themselves so that they have scribe(s), spokespeople and researchers for different areas, such as feeding, grooming, costs, housing and exercise.
● Using the information sheets, books and Internet, challenge to prepare a case in favour of having a pet.
They will need to consider how to care for it and how to counteract arguments. They must be able to support their opinion with researched facts and consider practicalities such as holidays and vet's bills.
● Explain that they will be making a group presentation to an imaginary parent who is against having a pet. They have to try to convince the parent that they will take responsibility for caring for the animal themselves.
● Suggest making props such as pictures, posters and pet-care information leaflets as visual aids to support their case. They might even present part of their case as an interview with the breeder of their chosen pet.
● Encourage the children to create notes as reminders of their argument. Remind them how to use emotive language to, for example, create a name for their proposed pet and a pseudo-personality. Demonstrate use of rhetorical language: 'Wouldn't it be soothing to go to sleep to the gentle trundle of a hamster in its wheel?', and demonstrate how to exploit sentimentality.
● After some preparation time, ask each group in turn to present their case. The rest of the class should take on the parental role, listening to the presentation, asking questions and pointing out potential problems for the groups to respond to.
● Close each presentation with a 'Yes' or 'No' vote from the listeners. As 'good parents' they must base their decision not on the animal or children per se, but on the strength of argument and power of presentation. Was it convincing? Was it persuasive? Did they answer questions? After the votes have been cast, ask individual 'parents' how they voted and why.

Differentiation
Nominate specific pets for younger children. Encourage older children to consider both sides of the argument by thinking of solutions to problems such as allergies, other pets, smells and so on.

AGE RANGE 8–11

LEARNING OBJECTIVE
To use discussion and group roles to organise and plan a collaborative activity.

CURRICULUM LINKS
NLS: Y4, T1–2; Y5, T1; Y6, T3.

Game on

What you need
A list of PE equipment available for school use; A3 paper; the 'Game on' photocopiable sheet on page 73.

What to do
● Make enough copies of the photocopiable sheet to allow one for each child plus several extras.
● Divide the class into planning groups. Allocate roles within each group: a leader, scribe to take notes, reporter, mentor, timetable-scribe and certificate designer.
● Tell the groups that the objective of their discussion is to plan a games afternoon for their class. They will need to plan a variety of activities, in sequence or in parallel, for a duration of 60 minutes.
● As they plan the content and running order they will need to consider:
    differing skills
    warm-up activities
    balance of more and less energetic games
    individual and team challenges
    supervisory roles, such as judges and
    equipment supervisors
    breaks
    safety and first-aid arrangements.
● Let the children design attendance awards for all participants using the photocopiable sheets as templates. Explain that the details of the recipient can be filled in on the day
● Advise children that they need to collate the information, considering what participants will need to know in advance. This will include details of venue, start and finish times, timetable, suitable clothing and so on.
● Tell the children that you will be looking for fun, variety and broad appeal. Their activities should include a range of skills including running, jumping, balancing and throwing. Give each group a list of PE equipment that they will be able to make use of on the day.
● After some time for discussion, ask the timetable-scribes to produce an outline timetable as a visual aid.
● Give each group another copy of the photocopiable sheet and explain that this will be a special award just from their group. Let the group work together to decide what the certificate will be awarded for and how it will be decorated. The certificate designers in each group can then work on the illustrations, border and content of their group's certificate.
● Ask reporters to present their group's plan to the rest of the class. Invite constructive feedback from others, offering improvements or adaptations and suggesting alternatives if necessary.

Differentiation
Limit the duration to 30 minutes for younger children. Challenge older children to plan for larger numbers, such as a parallel class.

Speaking and
Listening Games

AGE RANGE 9–11

LEARNING OBJECTIVE
To analyse and discuss how given texts work after reading them together; to share ideas to develop patterned dialogue and present it to other groups.

CURRICULUM LINKS
NLS: Y5, T2; Y6, T2.

Ad infinitum

What you need
The 'Ad infinitum' photocopiable sheet on page 74 (one per pair of children); pencils; paper.

What to do
● Ask the children to organise themselves into pairs. Give each pair a copy of the 'Ad infinitum' photocopiable sheet. Allow time for the children to read the verses and discuss the form of verse with their partner. It may be necessary to call a halt to the reading as they can go on for ever!

● Can the children recognise the word-play of 'hoodoo' and 'who do'? Discuss the expression 'to carry on till the cows come home', explaining that it is a metaphorical term for 'all day' or 'a very long time' and talk about its combined literal use in this verse.

● Challenge the children to read the rhyme about Michael Finnigan in such a way that all the lines rhyme, for example, running 'begin again' together to sound like 'beginnigan'.

● Encourage the children to perform the verses to the class. Pre-arrange a hand-signal to bring them to a stop.

● Sort the children into groups and ask them to brainstorm ideas for a short, circular story-poem of this kind. They can be for one or more voices but should end as they began with the opportunity to continue indefinitely. Take the opportunity to introduce the Latin term *ad infinitum*, meaning 'for ever'.

● Hear the children's draft poems and invite suggestions for reworking and refining. Invite the rest of the class to join in when they know the words.

Differentiation
With younger children, offer common phrases as a starting point. For example, 'Well, blow me down!' or 'Say again…!'. Challenge older children to compose a poem for several voices.

Cause and effect

● Sometimes, when we are young, we make up our own superstitions.

● As we grow older we know that these were funny and do not really matter. Try making up endings to the following. Decide whether they might be lucky or unlucky. Is there any common sense to them?

If you drop your pencil, then _____

Pick a daisy and _____

● Make up more silly superstitions about everyday events, but remember, they are made up – don't believe them!

_____

_____

_____

● Swap ideas with a friend. Think up an action that will counteract the bad luck, like throwing spilt salt over your left shoulder.

The Red Arrows

Have you ever watched a stunt kite flying in the wind? It will suddenly dive like a bird scooping to catch its prey. Then it will climb again, high into the sky. Sometimes it will weave up and down following a zigzag course and loop the loop, before it swoops, spiralling down in a twisting roll. Then, again, it will turn sharply to zoom up vertically over your head. It is an amazing sight.

While the kite dances in the sky, its flyers have both feet firmly on the ground. They control the kite skilfully, as they pull and jerk the string. The flight of the kite is graceful and beautiful to watch. And if something goes wrong, only the kite will plummet to earth; its controllers will still be standing safely on the ground. No broken bones; only their pride may be hurt.

Now, imagine instead that the super stunt kite is actually a group of nine aeroplanes. Picture them flying in tight formation in the shape of a diamond. As they fly, each movement is matched so perfectly with that of the next plane, that they appear to move as one. The aircraft fly so close together that they seem to be joined by invisible strings. They look like a bright red kite performing stunts. But, unlike a kite, there are real live pilots sitting proudly at the controls. They make sure every whooshing turn and whizzing twist; each spinning plunge and big-dipper rise, is synchronised. Now you are close to imagining an air-display by The Red Arrows, the Royal Air Force Aerobatic Team. There are over 100 members of the squadron, men and women, and team-members will take turns to pilot the aircraft.

It takes great skill and bravery to be part of the Red Arrows display team. As the pilots of nine Hawk aircraft carve their wonderful paths across the sky they make it look easy, as if they really were a carefree kite or a bird, free to enjoy riding the thermals. In fact it takes discipline, dedication and hours of team work and practice to achieve their exciting formation flying. It is exhilarating to watch the aircraft, now moving as one; now peeling off one by one, in perfect timing, to fly separate paths. A minute later, round they come again to reform seamlessly as one, while splendidly colourful vapour trails sign the sky with the team's spectacular autograph of perfection.

© Celia Warren

Tabletop game

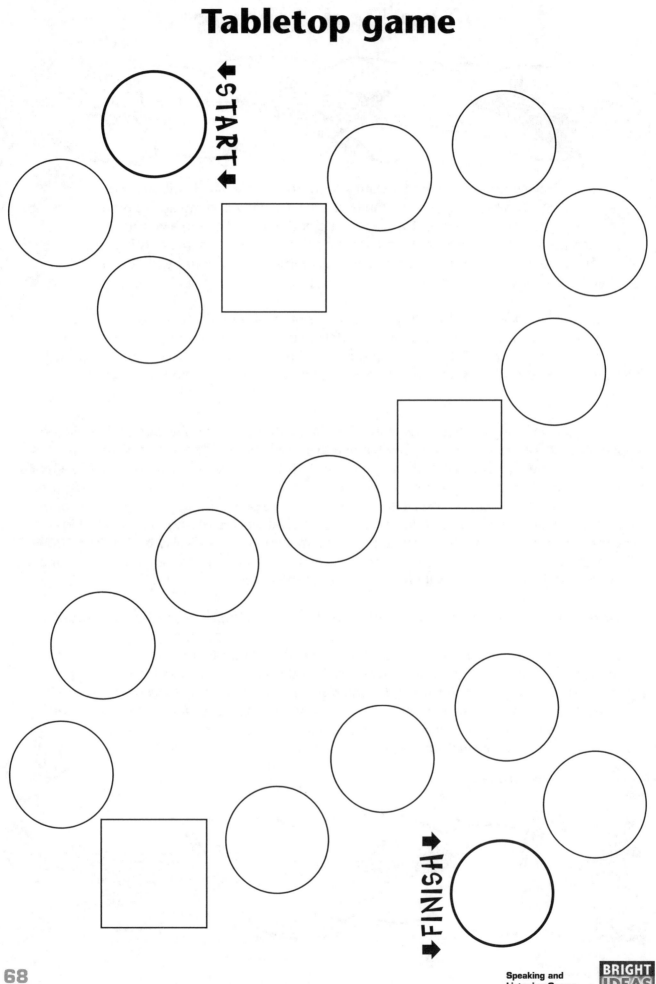

Speaking and
Listening Games

Have you packed?

Teddy, Toothbrush, Toothpaste

Name _____

Score | | |

Same poet, different poem

Summer Sun

Yes,
the sun shines
bright
in the summer,
and the breeze
is soft
as a sigh.

Yes,
the days are
long
in the summer,
and the sun
is King
of the sky.

© Wes Magee

Calling, calling

The sky is grey
And flakes are falling.
I hear the snowmen
Calling, calling

Outside it's wild.
Dad's car is st-st-stalling.
Next door my friends are
Calling, calling

Sliding, sledging
And, oh, snowballing!
The winter winds are
Calling, calling.

© Wes Magee

Speaking and
Listening Games

Compare and contrast

Canute's Account

Looked really cute in my new bathing suit so today I thought I'd go with my courtiers down to the beach.

They kept making speeches to flatter me, how I was so powerful I could subdue anything. Phew!

Well, enough's enough. I called their bluff: ordered a chair and sat down there at the edge of the sea and shouted, 'Sea! I, King Canute, proclaim it your duty to stop just where you are. Right there.'

The tide rose and rose till it reached my toes, then my robe trimmed with furs, so I said, 'Well sirs, it appears you're mistaken ...' But they'd all taken themselves out of reach way up the beach.

Taught them not to talk so much rot! But I'm sneezing a lot now and think I have got a cold.

Letter to My Uncle

Dear Uncle,

1912, the 17th of March

Thank you for your invitation to sail with you next month. I'd very much like to accept but there's a complication – I really ought to write and ask my parents. They may not let me miss more time from school after my illness. So, with your forbearance, I'll write. But stopping me would be too cruel!

I hear that the TITANIC's really something – the biggest thing afloat, that's what they say. Her maiden voyage! And I could be coming. If they say no, I think I'll stow away! Perhaps there's hope though. Maybe they'll agree. I'll let you know.

Your loving nephew, G.

© Jill Townsend

Myth and material

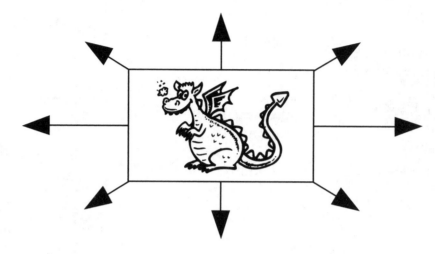

stone	silver	brick	clay	stone
water	wood	paper	sand	steel	glass

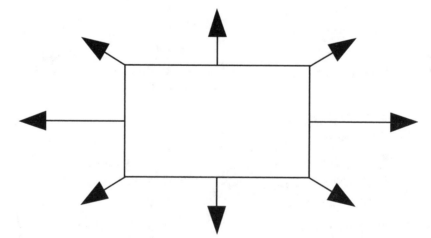

Speaking and
Listening Games

**BRIGHT
IDEAS**

Game on

Certificate of

....

Awarded to

....

....

....

Ad infinitum

● Read these verses aloud with a partner. Alternate lines and start again with line one as your partner finishes the last line. Do they ever end?

There was an old man called Michael Finnigan,
He grew whiskers on his chinnigan,
The wind came out and blew them in again,
Poor old Michael Finnigan, begin again.
There was an old man called Michael Finnigan…

I like watching cows.
I could watch cows till the cows come home.
But the cows never will come home
As the cows never left home
As we have no cows!
Pity really, as
I like watching cows.
I could watch cows till the cows come home…

© Celia Warren

You remind me of the man.
        What man?
The man with the power.
        What power?
The power of hoodoo.
        Hoodoo?
You do.
        I do what?
You remind me of the man…

Speaking and
Listening Games

CHAPTER 4

Drama

AGE RANGE 7-9

LEARNING OBJECTIVE
To present character through dialogue to engage the interest of an audience; to understand the term 'adjective'.

CURRICULUM LINKS
NLS: Y3, T2; Y4, T2.

Pass the flag

What you need
Music-playing facilities; small flag (can be made from paper taped to a pencil); 23 small white cards; 23 small blue cards; two containers; lively music.

What to do
● Prepare the cards before the class begins. On each of the 23 white cards, write one of the following characters: postal worker, astronaut, farmer, shop keeper, market seller, newspaper delivery boy or girl, teenager, childminder, street musician, police officer, newsreader, clown, athlete, footballer, ballet dancer, builder, painter and decorator, receptionist, doctor, dentist, teacher, cleaner, cook.
● On each of the 23 blue cards, write one of the following moods: happy, cross, sad, excited, sleepy, bold, shy, angry, confused, preoccupied, tired, energetic, slow, impatient, sarcastic, annoyed, kind, generous, irritable, mean, spiteful, gentle, worried.
● Place each set of cards in a container.
● Seat the children in a circle and put the two containers of cards in the centre. Start the music and encourage the children to pass the flag around the circle. When you stop the music, whoever is holding the flag must go to the middle and, without looking, take one white and one blue card. They should then choose a partner to join them in the middle of the circle.
● They then have 30 seconds to discuss a scene which they should improvise using appropriate dialogue. So if they pick, for example, a 'cross childminder', they might say: 'Hold my hand when we cross the road' to their partner.
● The partner, who plays the 'child' might respond by holding a fold of the 'childminder's' clothing. The 'childminder' could say: 'I told you to hold my hand, not make my jacket sticky!', and the 'child' could respond 'But my hands aren't sticky!' and so on.
● After a minute, ask the actors to stop. Invite the rest of the group to guess what part the first child was playing. A guess of 'parent' might be allowed, as parents are childminders much of the time. A guess of 'bad-tempered' instead of 'cross' could be allowed as a near synonym.
● Ask the children to return to their places, leaving the cards next to their original containers. Start the music and play again.

Differentiation
Help to give younger children confidence by modelling characters and moods for them. Extend the vocabulary of more confident children by using more adventurous adjectives such as 'exasperated' or 'diffident'. Provide thesauruses and dictionaries.

Speaking and Listening Games

AGE RANGE 6–11

LEARNING OBJECTIVE
To present a situation and characters through dialogue and engage the interest of the audience.

CURRICULUM LINKS
NLS: Y2, T3; Y3, T1; Y4, T1; Y5, T1; Y6, T1.

Are we nearly there yet?

What you need
Four chairs.

What to do
● Tell the children that you are going to play a game called 'Are we nearly there yet?'. Ask whether anyone remembers saying those words on a long journey. Invite other suggestions of phrases that might be heard on a long journey, such as 'How many more miles?', 'I'm hungry' or 'I need the toilet'.
● Ask four children to come to the front, bringing their chairs with them. Arrange them like seats in a saloon car; two at the front and two at the back, and ask the children to sit on their chairs. Nominate one child as 'driver'.
● Invite the rest of the class to suggest who the four people might be, for example, parents and children, a taxi driver and three passengers or a car full of holiday-makers.
● Discuss the purpose of their journey. Perhaps it is a business or shopping trip. Maybe the car is carrying a bride and her bridesmaids on their way to a wedding.
● Among themselves, encourage the four children to choose their characters and a supposed destination. Explain that at least one of them must have a problem, such as being too hot so they want to open a window. Someone else in the car has a conflicting problem, for example, they don't want the widow open because of the draft.
● Ask the rest of the group if they can guess who in the car is happy. Who is cross? Why? Encourage the children in the car to give clues to answer such questions through their dialogue and manner. They must act their parts, improvising speech and gesture and using appropriate voices. For example, a grandparent might have a shaky voice and poor hearing, requiring others to raise their voice.
● Encourage the four children to create plausible dialogue, responding to what is said by the other occupants of the car. Suggest that they use humour to bring out the differences between the characters.
● The episode does not need a conclusion as it is an ongoing situation. After a few minutes, invite children in the audience to guess who the different characters are, from the actors' tone, manner, vocabulary and voice. Can they work out which are adults and which are children? Encourage them to explain their reasons.

Differentiation
Give less confident children specific scenarios and roles, and help them to create suitable voices and mannerisms. Challenge more confident children to develop their scenario into a humorous sketch, with a pay-off at the end.

AGE RANGE 5—9

LEARNING OBJECTIVE
To dramatise a story creating dialogue and increasing understanding of character, behaviour and setting.

CURRICULUM LINKS
NLS: Y1, T1–3; Y2, T1–3; Y3, T1–3; Y4, T1-3.

Growing thumbnails

What you need
The 'Growing thumbnails' photocopiable sheet on page 91 (one between two children); examples of Aesop's fables.

What to do
● Read the following retelling of one of Aesop's fables to the children:

The lion and the mouse
One day, a big lion was lying fast asleep, when he felt a tickle. He woke up and found a tiny mouse running up and down all over him. His paw came down hard on the mouse and he opened his huge mouth as if to eat him.

'Please forgive me, O king of the jungle,' cried the mouse. 'If you let me go I shall never forget it and maybe I will be able to help you one day.'

The lion roared with laughter at the thought of a tiny mouse helping him but he let the mouse go.

Some time later hunters came to the jungle and, before he knew it, the poor lion was caught in a trap. The hunters tied him up in a net made of thick ropes and left him. They planned to come back later and take him alive to put him on show in a cage. The lion was angry and afraid.

Just then, the little mouse came along and saw the lion's predicament.

'You are in a fix,' said the mouse, 'but you helped me to escape and I shall help you.' The mouse began to nibble and chew at the rope until the net fell apart and the lion was free.

'There,' said the mouse, 'I said one day I would help you, and I did.'

'Thank you, little mouse,' said the lion. 'You were right. Little friends may prove to be great friends.'

● Point out that as with all Aesop's fables, the story has a moral. Open the moral up to discussion, considering the fairness and unfairness of the situation at all stages. Identify the direct speech, rewriting the words in speech bubbles next to simple sketches of the lion and the mouse. Ask the children to read them in role as you retell the story.
● Distribute the photocopiable sheets between each pair of children. Explain that these are 'thumbnails' of the original story; they contain just the bare plot and no direct speech. Working in their pairs, ask the children to decide what the characters say to each other. Point out that what they say and how they say it will tell us something about the character's personality.
● Invite the children to act out the stories with their partners, speaking the lines they have written and / or improvising along similar lines.

Differentiation
Allow less confident readers to act out the story about the lion and the mouse. Encourage more confident children to paraphrase the existing dialogue and improvise more.

AGE RANGE 7–11

LEARNING OBJECTIVE
To use voice and gesture to explore fictitious characters through improvisation.

CURRICULUM LINKS
NLS: Y3, T2; Y4, T1; Y5, T1; Y6, T1.

Buttons and bows

What you need
Pencils; paper; a collection of small personal objects arranged on trays. These could be a variety of buttons, badges, a book of stamps, pens, pencils, hair-bobbles, hair-slides, hats, gloves, pens, combs, nail-clippers, sunglasses, purses, key-rings, old car-keys, tapes, tiny toys, small pictures of pets, people, houses and gardens (cut from magazines).

What to do
● Scatter the collected items on trays, choosing as wide a variety as possible to reflect a broad range of age, gender and occupation. Place the trays on tables around the room.

● Ask the children to wander around and look at the objects, discussing with friends who they might belong to. After a few minutes, ask children to select an item and take it back to their seat.

● Encourage them to handle the item and think about who it might belong to. How does it reflect the owner's personality? Ask them to imagine that they are that person. Why have they kept it? Where did it come from? What purpose does or will it have?

● Ask the children to make notes about the person, including their name, age, where they live and what they do, gradually creating a character.

● When the children have a basic idea of their character, encourage them to give the character a catch-phrase or a physical habit such as clearing their throat or scratching their nose. When do they exhibit these habits?
When they are nervous or worried?

● In pairs, invite the children to choose a scenario where each child's character meets. They must decide if they have met before or are meeting for the first time and improvise a conversation, conducting all dialogue in role.

● Encourage the children to act out other aspects of their meeting. If they are playing tennis, perhaps they chat over the net. If they are queuing in a supermarket, perhaps they discuss some product that they are buying for the first time.

● Explain that the item that was the springboard for their character does not need to feature in their scenario, although it may do so if they wish.

Differentiation
Help younger children to build their character. Encourage older children to add more background to their character, such as family members.

Dramatically speaking

AGE RANGE 8–10

LEARNING OBJECTIVE
To adopt different styles of speech pattern and voice, formal and informal and displaying state of mind; to understand the term 'adverb'.

CURRICULUM LINKS
NLS: Y4, T1; Y5, T1.

What you need
A safe, open space.

What to do
● Introduce adverbs to the children by thinking first of adjectives and then (usually) adding 'ly', for example, brisk(ly); calm(ly).
● Explain that we use adverbs to qualify the meanings of verbs. We can use them to make something happen or someone behave 'in the manner of the word'. Collect more examples and experiment with how they might be represented in speech.
● Demonstrate that the adverb itself might dictate our choice of words. So, telling the class to tidy up 'briskly' might be: 'Come along now! Everything away at once! Chop-chop, let's have the room spotless!' while 'calmly' might be interpreted: 'I want everybody to finish what they are doing and then begin to tidy up, making sure that the room is left spotlessly clean'.
● Ask one child to leave the room while the rest of the class chooses an adverb. If they are struggling, suggest that they choose from the following: pompously; quietly; breathlessly; hesitantly; boldly; fiercely; cautiously; abstractedly; politely; gently; aggressively.
● On the child's return, explain that you would like him or her to ask questions or requests of the rest of the group in order to find out what the chosen adverb is. The children who are questioned must answer, or carry out the request, in the manner of the adverb.
● Start by suggesting that the following requests are spoken in the manner of the adverb:
  1) recite a nursery rhyme
  2) say a times-table
  3) ask the way to the station
  4) say what you had for dinner
  5) read a paragraph from a book
  6) order a meal at a café

● Discuss the merits of individual children's performance. If a word was guessed quickly, was it perhaps too laboured and obvious a performance or was it skilful? If it was not guessed, was the performance or speech too obscure?

Differentiation
Prepare a few prompt lines for younger children to read or repeat in the manner of the word. Ask more confident children to take on a persona – famous or fictional – and to mimic the person as well as speaking in the manner of the word.

AGE RANGE 9-11

LEARNING OBJECTIVE
To adopt appropriate roles and consider alternative ways of interpreting text, recognising and understanding metaphor and figures of speech.

CURRICULUM LINKS
NLS Y5, T1-2; Y6, T2.

Proverbs

What you need
13 pieces of card for each group of children.

What to do
● Prepare by writing one of the following proverbs on each piece of card:
1) Absence makes the heart grow fonder
2) Pride comes before a fall
3) Out of sight, out of mind
4) Strike while the iron's hot
5) You scratch my back and I'll scratch yours
6) Look before you leap
7) Once bitten, twice shy
8) Many hands make light work
9) Too many cooks spoil the broth
10) More haste, less speed
11) Kill two birds with one stone
12) Better late than never
13) Wilful waste brings woeful want

● Choose two or three of the cards to read aloud to the children. Explain and compare their literal and metaphorical meanings. For example, the proverb 'You scratch my back and I'll scratch yours' has a literal meaning – performing mutual tasks to help each other in a mutually difficult position – which can be extended metaphorically to many situations in everyday life.
● Distribute the cards among the groups. Ask the children to choose one proverb and devise a story to demonstrate its meaning and the truth behind it.
● Explain that you would like them to improvise a dialogue to create a short sketch or dramatic scene. The rest of the class will try to guess which proverb they have chosen.
● Alternatively, they may create a freeze frame, highlighting the main message of their proverb-centred story, with all performers prepared to answer questions from the rest of the class.
● When the children offer guesses, encourage the actors to accept recognition of the spirit of meaning of the proverb and its message, even if it is worded unconventionally. For example, 'You help me and I'll help you' shows understanding of the back-scratching proverb. Remind children that the specific wording is a useful and universal 'shortcut' to state an opinion.

Differentiation
Ensure that younger children understand their chosen proverb before they begin planning their interpretation. Older children could work in pairs.

Speaking and
Listening Games

**BRIGHT
IDEAS**

AGE RANGE 8–11

LEARNING OBJECTIVE
To interpret a poem creating a realistic dialogue, considering the speakers' use of language, facial expression, gesture and voice.

CURRICULUM LINKS
NLS: Y4, T1; Y5, T2–3; Y6, T1–2.

Good news, bad news

What you need
The poem 'Wilkins' Drop' from the 'Good news, bad news' photocopiable sheet on page 92; card; art materials; scissors.

What to do
● Make one copy of the photocopiable sheet for each child.
● Read the poem 'Wilkins' Drop' aloud to the children, modelling appropriate pauses, emphasis, gesture and voice.
● Give each child a copy of the photocopiable sheet and invite an able reader to reread the poem while the rest of the class follow the text. Discuss and analyse the humorous effects; how the poet paints a graphic picture in words and uses our anticipation to prolong the tension and so increase and sustain the humour.
● Identify use of: phrases rather than full sentences; colloquial language ('a proper brute!'); rhyme to enhance the humour; metaphor ('earth comes rushing' – it is Wilkins who is moving).
● Ask the children, in pairs or small groups, to plan a performance of the poem. They may use visual aids, for example, one child could hold a cardboard cut-out of Wilkins and other props while the other reads or, preferably, recites the poem. Consider speaking it as a two-voice poem, with one child speaking the good / bad / better news 'announcement' lines and their partner the action lines.
● Return to the poem and, again in pairs or small groups, plan a presentation of the poem's content as a conversation between two people, one telling the other what happened. Consider the way that facial expressions and gesture can be used to highlight the drama of the event. Place the conversation in context by inviting one child to lie still on the floor, pretending to be Wilkins, listening to the conversation across him and only moving his eyes from one speaker to the other.

● Next, rehearse the poem as a news report, again considering how expression, voice and gesture can be used for this style of retelling.
● After rehearsing, present the performance to another class or in assembly. Use the performance to illustrate that good and bad things happen to us, that we need to take care of ourselves and that sometimes we may struggle to achieve our ambitions!

Differentiation
Help children to write and perform their own 'good news; bad news' story poem. Encourage more able children to underline sections of text in the poem with green, yellow and red pens, according to whether it is good, better or bad news.

AGE RANGE 5-9

LEARNING OBJECTIVE
To explore issues in role, extemporising to create realistic dialogue; to assess the performance of other groups; to consider strengths and weaknesses.

CURRICULUM LINKS
NLS: Y1, T2; Y2, T3; Y3, T3; Y4, T1.

Excuses, excuses!

What you need
A safe, open space.

What to do
● Point out that, as we go through life, we often find ourselves in situations where we have to explain and justify our action or inaction. If we haven't tidied our room or done our homework, our parent or teacher may demand to know why. It is then that we start coming up with excuses. Some are firmly justifiable; some are slight and insubstantial; some are downright lies! Some are believable and some totally implausible – whether true or not!

● Explain that today, the children are going to have fun with imaginative excuses. They do not need to be true as this is only a game, however they do have to be plausible. Explain the difference between an invented 'real life' scenario and 'fantasy'; their excuse could not be that they were dragged off to Mars by little green men in a flying saucer!

● Ask each child to find a partner or form a group of three. One must adopt the role of 'accuser' and the other the 'accused'. The 'accuser' will have to say what is amiss while the 'accused' will need to invent an excuse. The children may create characters and a scenario of their own or use or adapt one of the following:

Bus driver and passengers
The driver has passed the stop without picking up passengers; later they challenge him at the bus depot. How do they phrase their complaint? What was the impact on their plans and on their lives? What was the bus driver's excuse?

Child and parent
The child's been to the sweet shop on the way home from school instead of going straight home. The parent is worried and angry. What is the child's excuse? Does the parent explain his or her reaction? What is the consequence of the episode?

● After some practice, watch the performances and invite constructive criticism from fellow classmates. Could the performances have been improved? How? Perhaps the clarity could be improved, or greater diversity was needed to distinguish one character from the other. What was good about the performance? Was the choice of vocabulary appropriate to the adult and contrasting child characters? Was the timing and delivery of dialogue good? Did it flow without obvious pauses?

Differentiation
Work with individual children who are less confident. Prompt where necessary to draw out extra dialogue and information from them. Challenge older children to work out an outcome of the excuse.

Speaking and
Listening Games

AGE RANGE 8–11

LEARNING OBJECTIVE
To use freeze frames to explore a situation, characters and their interaction.

CURRICULUM LINKS
NLS: Y4, T1–3; Y5, T3; Y6, T1.

Eyewitness

What you need
A selection of everyday props from school and home, such as a football, tennis ball, skipping rope, books, a broom, racquet, skateboard; paper; pencils.

What to do
● Explain to the children that eyewitnesses are notoriously unreliable. People who think they remember what they saw are often mistaken. Demonstrate this by asking the children some questions. When came into class today, who did you speak to first? When you took the register, what colour was your pen?

● Next, ask questions about the children themselves. Who was first in the classroom this morning? Who opened the window? Was Leanne wearing her hair up or down yesterday?

● Explain that they are going to play two roles: actors and detectives. Ask the children to sort themselves into groups of five or six, and invite each group to select one or two props from the selection available.

● Explain that you would like them to invent an incident or accident that involves their prop. The characters must all be involved in a confrontation as a result of this incident; some directly, with clashing viewpoints and some acting as witnesses with varying degrees of reliability. Role-play the confrontation to explore the characters and situation. Decide what 'really' happened. Plan which eyewitness will be most accurate and how the other accounts may differ.

● Allow time for each group to plan their scenario. At this stage it does not need to have a resolution. It should centre on the event and its immediate aftermath and interaction between characters.There should be areas of contention and no clear culprit.

● Ask each group in turn to present a freeze-frame of the moment of crisis and tension.

● Invite the rest of the class to play 'detective', asking up to ten questions to help build up a picture of what happened. They will need to take notes to help them remember what the witnesses said. Remind the 'eyewitnesses' that some will report more accurately and others less so.

● Encourage the detectives to consider their notes and decide what happened and what might happen next. Through discussion, develop an outcome of the scenario. Ask each group in turn to close the exercise with a freeze-frame of the situation's outcome.

Differentiation
Provide a scenario for groups of less confident children, such as a child kicking a ball through their neighbour's window, while the neighbour is cutting down a hedge that would have stopped the ball. Ask more confident children to develop a short play with beginning, middle and end.

AGE RANGE 10–11

LEARNING OBJECTIVE
To investigate how characters are built up from small details; to recognise how poets manipulate words.

CURRICULUM LINKS
NLS: Y5, T1; Y6, T2-3.

The new kid

What you need
The poem 'The New Boy' on the photocopiable sheet on page 93; coloured pencils.

What to do
● Make one copy of the poem for each pair of children.
● Distribute the photocopiable sheets and ask the children to read the poem. Have they heard of Tarzan from the book by Edgar Rice Burroughs? Have they seen him in films or cartoons based on the book?
● In this poem, we learn the new boy's name in line two. Ask the children to underline in one colour any other clues as to the boy's identity (he climbs ropes, is met by a chimpanzee and so on).
● In the poem, Tarzan knows who he is, even if he can't spell his name! The other children know nothing about him, but want to find out more. Choose a different colour to underline words that show that the children want to welcome the new boy (…think he's brilliant; he leaves us standing (literally and metaphorically)).
● Invite four or five children to come to the front of the class. Allocate the role of Tarzan to one child, and his classmates to the others. Explain that, unlike in the poem, the Tarzan at the front of the class does NOT know his identity. Everything in this school is topsy-turvy and his classmates DO know his identity.
● Ask the 'classmates' to talk and behave as if they know who Tarzan is, without saying his name. The child playing Tarzan should act the part of a 'new boy'. Invite 'Tarzan' to ask questions that a new child might ask, such as 'Where do I hang my coat?' The others should respond as if they knew his habits, for example, 'Well I expect you're used to hanging it on the branch of a tree, but here we use pegs'.
● Ask the children to sit back down. Choose another child and ask him or her to leave the room for a few minutes while the rest of the class decide on a fictional character for the 'new kid', perhaps one from a school story. Repeat the activity. So, this time, the child might ask, 'Can I stay for school dinners', to which the response might be, 'This is a boarding school, silly. You stay here for all your meals'.
● Continue playing, so that every child can take a turn at guessing.

Differentiation
For younger children, limit the number of questions asked before guessing the persona. More confident groups could choose real people, either living or dead.

AGE RANGE 8-11

LEARNING OBJECTIVE
To adopt roles to explore and discuss feelings and behaviour and use conjecture to discuss possible outcomes; to understand figurative language.

CURRICULUM LINKS
NLS: Y4, T1-3; Y5, T1 & T3; Y6, T1-2.

What next?

What you need
The 'What next?' photocopiable sheet on page 94.

What to do
● Make one copy of the photocopiable sheet for each child.
● Distribute copies of the photocopiable sheet and ask the children to read the poem 'Left out' to themselves.
● Ask what emotions the speaker is feeling. Note that the emotions of anger, fear, distress and humiliation are not named as such. Look for similes and metaphors. Why are these stronger than simply saying, 'I feel angry and upset'?
● Can the children make their hands look like 'rocks' in their pocket? What emotions make us clench our fists? Ask individuals to act the part of the child as you re-read the poem, using gesture, body and facial language.

● Consider possible causes of the situation, drawing the children's attention to the title of the poem.
● Ask the children to consider the other people in the poem. How are they behaving? What emotions are they feeling? If we were in their position how might we behave? Would we have the courage to distance ourselves from the bullies and stand up for the child who's left out?
● Ask the children if they have had similar experiences. Organise them into groups and ask them to discuss what might happen next. Allow time for discussion and for children to choose roles within the scenario. Explain that you would like them to create a freeze-frame of what happens next. For example, this might involve one child standing apart from the group, another child with their arm around the first, and a third child walking towards them. Would this be a conciliatory move? Perhaps they see it as threatening?
● Explain to the groups that, while they are in their freeze-frames, the rest of the class will be directing questions towards the characters.
● Choose one group to start. Begin by asking questions such as, 'Why have you got your arm around her?'; 'Where are you going?'; 'Why?'; 'How are you feeling right now?'; 'Do you feel better or worse than you did a minute ago?'. The children in the freeze-frame must answer the questions in role, with realistic dialogue.
● Compare how the groups resolved the situation. How might it have been avoided in the first place?

Differentiation
Provide ideas for settings, such as in the playground, to help younger children begin their discussion. Ask more able children to invent metaphors from the point of view of the others in the poem, expressing emotions such as regret, remorse and guilt.

Making headlines

AGE RANGE 7–11

LEARNING OBJECTIVE
To develop fictitious characters and plots; to create and resolve a conflict of interests, improvising dialogue between two characters; to secure basic knowledge of alphabetical order.

CURRICULUM LINKS
NLS: Y3, T1-2; Y4, T1& T3; Y5, T3; Y6, T1.

What you need
Paper; pencils; a selection of newspaper headlines; alphabet frieze.

What to do
● Explain that you would like the children to invent newspaper headlines to act as a story stimulus. Show them examples of simple headlines or list the following examples:
Clown Makes Money for Nurses
Princess Visits Homeless
Lorry Drivers Stop Mayor's Progress
Climber Follows Father's Footsteps

● Draw the children's attention to the brevity of the headlines. Note which important words are included and which omitted, showing their construction to be different from complete sentences. Discuss which headlines imply conflict and which co-operation.
● Display an alphabet frieze. Explain the meaning of 'consecutive' and then ask the children to choose four consecutive letters from the frieze. Challenge them to create their own headlines using the four consecutive letters, for example:
Crocodile **D**iscusses **E**ating **F**riend
Student **T**akes **U**ndertaker's **V**an
● Working in pairs, encourage the children to think broadly of at least two characters, taking inspiration from the letters, to create a headline that suggests conflict. Draw on jobs and professions, animals, mythical beasts and made-up characters, such as martians. Alternatively, involve a character from history, for example: 'Evangelical Finds Galileo Heretic'.
● Consider how conversations consist of questions and answers, expression of feelings, opinions, facts, beliefs and value judgements. When does a conversation become a debate? When does a debate become an argument? When people argue, do they speak in full sentences?
● In pairs, ask the children to contribute suggestions as to what one character might say to another. How will their choice of vocabulary and voice, manner and facial expression, reflect the character? Will any character have a catchphrase or idiosyncratic speech patterns? Challenge the children to ask and answer questions of the characters in role as they begin to act out the headline situation that they are creating. Where does the conversation lead? What will happen next? What is the final result?
● Choose pairs to perform their script to the rest of the class. Observe how the children's portrayal, in dialogue and manner, highlights differences between the characters.
● Invite feedback from the rest of the class. Make sure that it is constructive and considers the whole performance, gesture, expression, tone of voice and clarity, as well as dialogue.

Differentiation
Help younger children to create headlines and discuss characters, and scribe the characters' opening words. Take the role of one of the characters to help them get started. More able children could develop written scripts into short plays developing character and plot.

AGE RANGE 5–7

LEARNING OBJECTIVE
To create roles showing different viewpoints
extemporising realistic dialogue.

CURRICULUM LINKS
NLS: Y1, T1–2; Y2, T1.

I want never gets!

What you need
A safe, open space.

What to do
● Begin by discussing the saying, 'I want never gets!'. Talk about its meaning. Decide on other ways of expressing a need or desire other than beginning, 'I want…'. Ask the children to imagine that they are in a situation where they want something but need the other person's agreement to get it, for example, 'I want …

Mum to buy me an ice-cream
to have a birthday party
my friend to lend me something or let me 'have a go'
to go on an outing or a special treat
to have more pocket money
swimming lessons
to be in a football team'.

● Ask the children to find a partner. Explain that they are going to act out scenarios where one child will be the person that wants something, and the other will be the potential provider. Invite them to decide who will play each role to start with.
● Remind the children that simply saying, 'I want…' will not help them to get their way or achieve their ambition. Advise them to use persuasive language and tactics to win the other person over. Warn the providers that they must, at first, resist and think up counter-arguments why they will not give in.
● Encourage the children to improvise their conversations in role and see where it leads them. Ask them to decide which argument will convince the provider that the child can have what he or she wants.
● After experimental time, invite the children to act out their conversation to the rest of the class. Invite the class to comment on how convincing each character was and why.

Differentiation
Delegate roles and designate a situation for younger children to explore through improvisation. Invite older children to develop their dialogue into a short play.

AGE RANGE 5–9

LEARNING OBJECTIVE
To create roles showing how behaviour can be interpreted from different viewpoints; to present events and dialogue between two characters, bringing out the differences between them; to comment constructively.

CURRICULUM LINKS
NLS: Y1, T1; Y2, T1; Y3, T1-2; Y4, T1-3.

Every picture tells a story

What you need
A safe, open space; the 'Every picture tells a story' photocopiable sheet on page 95.

What to do
● Make one copy of the photocopiable sheet for each pair of children. Distribute the sheets and look at the pictures together.
● Explain that the pictures show conflicts between two people. In pairs, ask the children to discuss what is happening in each picture. Hear some of their interpretations, and invite comments and suggestions from others.
● Ask the children to support their opinions with evidence from the pictures, such as the characters' facial expressions, stance and position and factors beyond the people. For instance, can anyone suggest why the child in the first picture is looking angry? What does the parent want? Argue each point of view. The child could be saying: 'I will look ridiculous!'; the adult might be saying: 'But everyone else will be dressed smartly'.
● After discussion, ask each pair to choose a scenario based on one of the pictures. Encourage each child to adopt a role from the picture and to improvise a dialogue. Explain that, on your signal, you would like them to swap roles. Encourage them to use facial expression, body language and gesture as part of their role-playing.
● Watch some of the performances. Ask the rest of the class to offer their opinions on the realism of the dialogue. How did the children make the adult's speeches sound different from the child's?

● Encourage each pair to discuss what happened next in their scenario . They will need to decide on a solution or compromise that brings closure to the situation. How can the two be reconciled?
● When the children have had time to plan an ending, ask them to start from the beginning, in role. When you give the signal, this time, it will be a sign for one of them to back down and the other to be persuaded to be accommodating, or whatever solution the children have planned to happen next.
● Finally, watch some of the scenes all the way through, inviting constructive comments from the rest of the class.

Differentiation
Allow younger children to write down their opening lines to give them confidence to continue without a script. Challenge older children to experiment with varying pitch and tone to give more realism to their characters.

AGE RANGE 9–11

LEARNING OBJECTIVE
To plan a presentation using appropriate language and oral techniques; to understand how audiences may be influenced by use of emotive language; to compare active and passive tense.

CURRICULUM LINKS
NLS: Y5, T1-3; Y6, T1-T3.

News and views

What you need
Traditional nursery rhyme and fairy tale texts; the 'News and views' photocopiable sheet on page 96; pencils.

What to do
● Invite the children to consider the emotive use of language by reporters. Offer examples:
using the word 'admitted' or 'confessed' rather than 'said'
using the passive tense, especially for conjecture ('it is thought that…' or 'it is expected…')
using generalised, unsubstantiated statements ('neighbours were amazed…' or 'teachers believe…') to support spurious facts
using alarmist language ('people fear that…')
using rhetorical questions ('Is it safe to go shopping alone?').
● Explain that you would like the children to choose a fairy tale or nursery rhyme to present as an emotive news item. They will need to begin with an attention-grabbing headline or title, for example: 'Whose pie was it anyway?'.
● Model a news report based on the story of Cinderella, using passive tense, rhetorical language and emotive words:

Motherless beauty used as skivvy!
Who would have thought that this beauty could be so abused? The world's anger is directed at the mistress of this house of cruelty, where an innocent young girl was so mistreated by her cruel stepmother. Happily, the gentle, caring Cinderella has gone from rags to riches as she prepares to wed her devoted Prince Charming. While they enjoy an emotional reunion – Yes! the shoe fitted! – the two ugly sisters have gone into hiding. Our reporters have caught up with them on a remote island…

● Working in pairs, encourage the children to choose a fairy tale or nursery rhyme from the selection of books.
● Give each pair of children a photocopiable sheet. Encourage them to work together to fill in the sheets, writing down key points from which they can construct a television or radio news report.
● When everyone has planned their report, invite pairs of children to perform them to the rest of the group.
● During each pair's performance, ask the rest of the class to listen carefully and be ready to answer questions as 'members of the crowd'. For example, 'Sanjit, what is your reaction to the news?'; 'Emma, you lived next door to Cinderella; how did she react when her father remarried?'
● Encourage the children to relax into their role-play and have fun.

Differentiation
Provide a toy microphone for younger children to use as a prop. More able children could script interviews with witnesses, bystanders, victims and perpetrators.

AGE RANGE 9–11

LEARNING OBJECTIVE
To develop scripts based on research and collected data; to discuss and assign roles; to increase understanding of past and present tense.

CURRICULUM LINKS
NLS: Y5, T1; Y6, T1&T3.

This was your life

What you need
Historical research resources and books; encyclopaedias; access to the Internet; hole-punch; A4 ring-binder; A4 paper; access to computer and printer if possible.

What to do
● Allow time in your planning for a preparation session and a presentation session for this activity.
● Choose a character from history, preferably within a topic that you are currently studying. Explain that you would like the children to present a tribute to a famous historical character as if they, and their contemporaries, were still alive. They will need teams to research individual contemporaries, friends and relatives and significant events during the character's life.
● Choose a volunteer to play the central role of the historical character whose life is being celebrated. (He or she will also help with research.)
● Nominate a presenter who, together with a group of assistants, will arrange how to present the story of the character's life. They will need to plan introductory scripts and links between 'guests' and an appropriate chronological 'running order', related to significant events in the central character's life. They will also need to write scripts for brief introductions to each character, giving clues of their identity before naming them. For example, 'Your Scottish cousin whom you sent to prison… it's Mary!'.
● Urge the children to have fun with the past and present tense, presenting the past as if it were the present with suitable dramatic licence. For example, 'Yes, Bess, this is your dear old Dad, Henry! Unfortunately your mother couldn't make it!' and ending, 'Yes, Good Queen Bess, this WAS your life!'.

● Arrange a group of two or three researchers to investigate each guest appearing. In each group, designate the role of the person being researched, such as Sir Francis Drake, and encourage each 'guest' to help research their own character.
● Researchers should produce a separate A4 page for each 'guest' or historical figure, telling a short anecdote about each and giving a copy to both the child playing the part and to the presenter. Type up and print off the pages, then put them in chronological order in the ring binder.
● Once sufficient information has been gathered, and the ring binder is complete, have fun hosting your very own version of 'This WAS your life'!

Differentiation
Involve less confident children to take part in 'crowd scenes', playing, for example, roles of gaolers or executioners at The Tower of London. Encourage older children to make props to support their performances.

Growing thumbnails

The fox and the crow

A fox saw a crow fly to the top of a tree with a piece of cheese in its beak. The fox wanted the cheese so he began to say flattering things to the crow. At last, he suggested that the crow must have a wonderful voice and asked her to sing.

The crow was very flattered but as soon as she opened her beak to sing, she dropped the cheese. It fell to the ground where fox snapped it up. He thanked the crow for the cheese and told her that she should never listen to people who flatter her.

© Celia Warren

The ant and the grasshopper

One summer's day a grasshopper was hopping around, playing and singing. An ant went by, carrying a heavy load of grain. The grasshopper asked the ant to stop and play and chat with him. The ant wouldn't stop because he was collecting stores of food for winter. The grasshopper thought that was a waste of time and carried on playing.

Later in the year, one winter's day, the grasshopper had nothing to eat and was starving. He saw the ant eating the grain that he collected and stored in the summer. The grasshopper knew that he too should have stocked up and got ready for the winter, but it was too late.

© Celia Warren

Good news, bad news

Wilkins' Drop

Great news!
To fulfil a lifelong ambition
Wilkins jumps from a plane;
Makes a slight omission
That's not such good news,
In fact, a proper brute:
What's missing is
His parachute.
Better news, though,
As earth comes rushing:
Haystack below –
Possible cushion.
Bad news again:
Embedded in stack –
Pitchfork with prongs
As sharp as a tack.
Good news:
Misses pitchfork. Phew!
Bad news:
Misses haystack too.

© Eric Finney

Speaking and Listening Games

The new kid

The New Boy

We've got a new boy in our class,
Tarzan is his name.
He's never been to school before;
To him it's all a game.
When Tarzan tries technology
He's all fingers and thumbs.
He signs his name 'Nazrat'
And he can't do simple sums.
Our teacher shakes her head at him
And sighs – she's lost all hope,
But we think Tarzan's brilliant
The way he climbs a rope.
Subtraction has him floundering,
He's not the world's best adder,
But he just leaves us standing
When he swings on our rope-ladder.

At home time at the school gate
With all the dads and mums
A chimpanzee meets Tarzan
Or an old ape sometimes comes.
Tarzan's still The New Boy
Yet I'm sure he'll soon make friends,
All the boys ask him to play
When the school-day ends.
They want to play at his house
In the jungle up a tree,
And all for just one reason
As far as I can see.
It's not that Tarzan's clever,
I hardly need explain,
He isn't good at football but
The boys ALL fancy Jane!

© Celia Warren

What next?

Left out
It feels as if pins
Are pricking my eyes.
My face is burning hot.
A firework is trying
To go off inside me.
My feet are glued to the spot.
My hands are rocks in my pockets.
I want to run away,

But my legs are rooted to the ground
Like trees. I have to stay
And listen
To everyone calling me names
And not letting me
Join in with their games.

© Celia Warren

Speaking and
Listening Games

BRIGHT
IDEAS

Every picture tells a story

News and views

EXCLUSIVELY MADE UP

DAILY GOSSIP

Original story or nursery rhyme: _____

Headline: _____

Central character: _____

Others involved: _____

_____

Background: What has just happened? _____

_____

_____

_____

Speaking and
Listening Games